r guide

Lincolnshire
and the Wolds

WALKS

Compiled by
Brian Conduit
Fully revised by
Neil Coates

D1556389

JARROLD
publishing

Text: Brian Conduit
                       Revised text for 2008 edition,
                       Neil Coates
Photography: Brian Conduit, Neil Coates
Editorial: Ark Creative (UK) Ltd
Design: Ark Creative (UK) Ltd

Series Consultant: Brian Conduit

OS Ordnance Survey® This product includes mapping data licensed from Ordnance Survey® with the permission of the Controller of Her Majesty's Stationery Office. © Crown Copyright 2008. All rights reserved. Licence number 100017593. Pathfinder is a registered trade mark of Ordnance Survey, the national mapping agency of Great Britain.

Jarrold Publishing   ISBN 978-0-7117-4986-3

While every care has been taken to ensure the accuracy of the route directions, the publishers cannot accept responsibility for errors or omissions, or for changes in details given. The countryside is not static: hedges and fences can be removed, field boundaries can be altered, footpaths can be rerouted and changes in ownership can result in the closure or diversion of some concessionary paths. Also, paths that are easy and pleasant for walking in fine conditions may become slippery, muddy and difficult in wet weather, while stepping stones across rivers and streams may become impassable.

If you find an inaccuracy in either the text or maps, please write to or e-mail Jarrold Publishing at the addresses below.

First published 2002 by Jarrold Publishing
Revised and reprinted 2008.

Printed in Belgium. 2/08

Pitkin Publishing Ltd,
Healey House, Dene Road, Andover, Ha
e-mail: info@totalwalking.co.uk
www.totalwalking.co.uk

Front cover: Lincoln Cathedral
Previous page: The two churches of Al

Nottinghamshire County Council Community Services	
Askews	
914.253	£10.99

Contents

Short, easy walks

Walks of modest length, likely to involve some modest uphill walking

More challenging walks which may be longer and/or over more rugged terrain, often with some stiff climbs

Keymap 1

Keymap 1

SCALE 1:333 333 or 1 INCH to about 5¼ MILES *1CM to 3.3KM*

KILOMETRES
0 2 4 6 8 10 15

MILES
0 2 4 6 8 10

SPOT HEIGHTS SHOWN IN METRES

Keymap 2

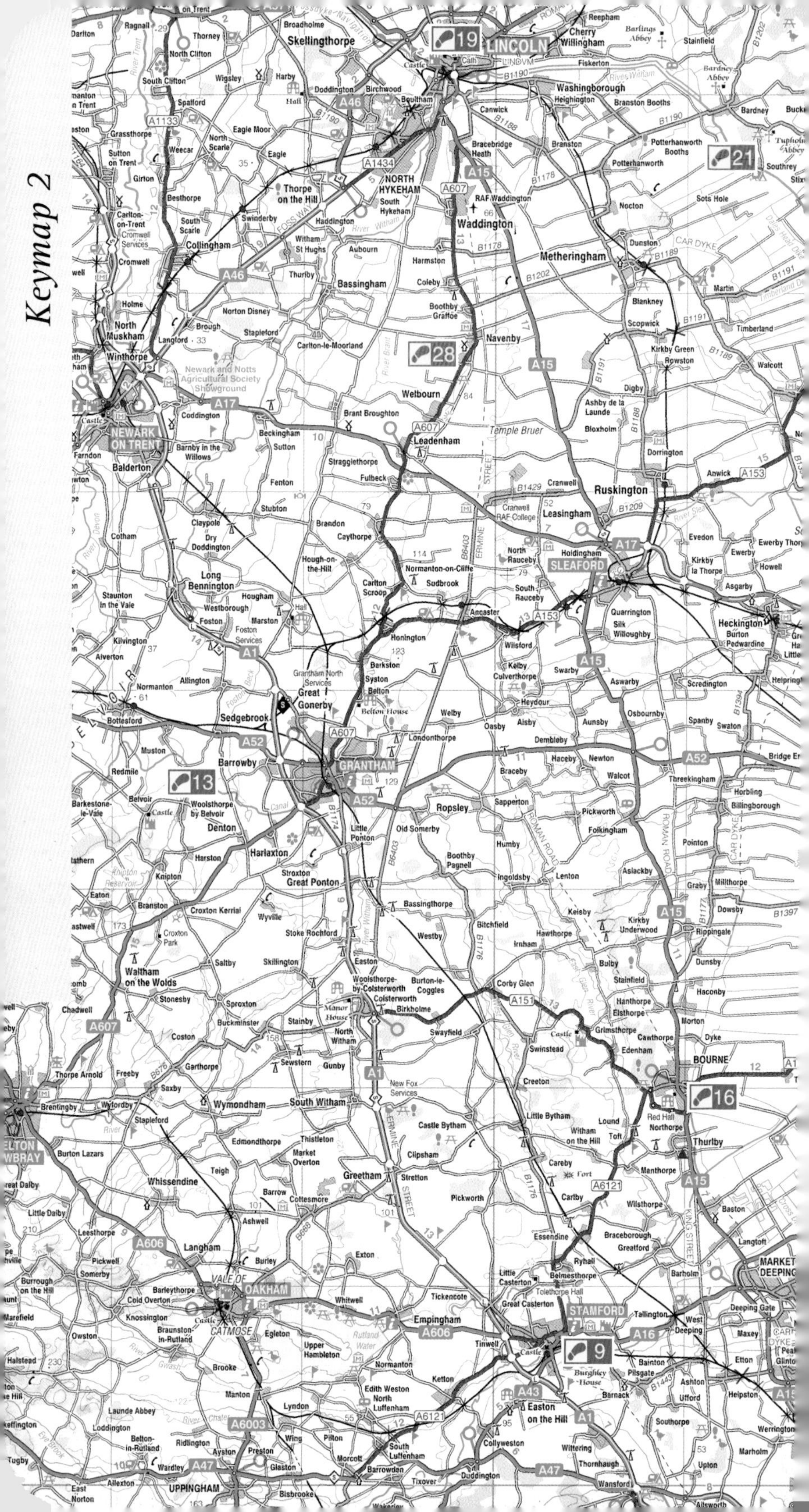
LINCOLN
19
Skellingthorpe
Cherry Willingham
Washingborough
Branston
NORTH HYKEHAM
Waddington
Metheringham
Bassingham
Collingham
Navenby
28
21
NEWARK ON TRENT
Balderton
Winthorpe
North Muskham
Newark and Notts Agricultural Society Showground
Welbourn
Leadenham
Brant Broughton
Ruskington
Leasingham
SLEAFORD
Cranwell
Fulbeck
Caythorpe
Long Bennington
Heckington
Ancaster
Great Gonerby
Belton House
GRANTHAM
Barrowby
Sedgebrook
Bottesford
13
Harlaxton
Denton
Great Ponton
Ropsley
Colsterworth
Corby Glen
BOURNE
16
Thurlby
South Witham
Wymondham
Greetham
Langham
OAKHAM
Empingham
STAMFORD
9
Burghley House
MARKET DEEPING
Deeping Gate
West Deeping
UPPINGHAM
Easton on the Hill
Ketton
Edith Weston
Rutland Water
Whissendine
Cottesmore
Castle Bytham
Tinwell
Barnack
Helpston
Wansford

SCALE 1:333 333 or 1 INCH to about 5¼ MILES *1CM to 3.3KM*

0 2 4 6 8 10 KILOMETRES 15

0 2 4 MILES 8 10

SPOT HEIGHTS SHOWN IN METRES

At-a-glance...

Walk	Page	Start	Nat. Grid Reference	Distance	Time	Highest Point
Alvingham and the Louth Canal	14	Alvingham Mill	TF 366913	3½ miles (5.6km)	1½ hrs	33ft (10m)
Around Horncastle	74	Horncastle	TF 258696	9 miles (14.5km)	4 hrs	213ft (65m)
Barnetby le Wold, Bigby and Somerby	71	Barnetby le Wold	TA 056098	6¾ miles (10.9km)	3 hrs	295ft (90m)
Barton and the River Humber	24	Barton Waterside, Clay Pits car park	TA 027233	5½ miles (8.9km)	2½ hrs	95ft (29m)
Boston and the River Witham	34	Market Place, Boston	TF 327441	6½ miles (10.5km)	3 hrs	16ft (5m)
Bourne Wood and Edenham	50	Bourne	TF 095201	6½ miles (10.5km)	3 hrs	200ft (61m)
Chapel St Leonards, Hogsthorpe and Chapel Point	53	Chapel St Leonards	TF 561722	7 miles (11.3km)	3½ hrs	39ft (12m)
Claythorpe Mill and the Swaby valley	28	Aby village hall	TF 412783	5½ miles (8.9km)	2½ hrs	154ft (47m)
Crowland and the River Welland	68	Crowland	TF 239102	8½ miles (13.7km)	4 hrs	20ft (6m)
Donington and the Bain valley	44	Donington on Bain	TF 235829	5½ miles (8.9km)	3 hrs	476ft (145m)
Four Lincoln Edge villages	87	Wellingore	SK 981568	8½ miles (13.7km)	4 hrs	246ft (75m)
Frampton Marsh	40	Frampton Marsh	TF 363384	6¾ miles (10.9km)	3 hrs	23ft (7m)
Guy's Head	20	Guy's Head	TF 491256	3¾ miles (6km)	2 hrs	23ft (7m)
Isle of Axholme	37	Epworth, Church Walk car park	SE 783039	6½ miles (10.5km)	3 hrs	98ft (30m)
Laceby, Irby upon Humber and Aylesby	84	Laceby	TA 213065	7¾ miles (12.5km)	3½ hrs	230ft (70m)
Lincoln and the Fossdyke	59	Castle Hill, Lincoln	SK 976718	7½ miles (12.1km)	3½ hrs	220ft (67m)
North Carlton and Scampton	22	Till Bridge Lane Viewpoint, A1500/B1398	SK 954783	4½ miles (7.2km)	2 hrs	184ft (56m)
Old Bolingbroke and East Keal	56	Old Bolingbroke	TF 348651	5¾ miles (9.3km)	3 hrs	305ft (93m)
Southrey, Bardney and Tupholme Abbey	65	Ferry Road, Southrey	TF 138663	8½ miles (13.7km)	4 hrs	33ft (10m)
Stamford, Easton on the Hill and Tinwell	31	Red Lion Square, Stamford	TF 029070	5½ miles (8.9km)	2½ hrs	289ft 88m
Tattershall and Coningsby	16	Tattershall	TF 212579	3½ miles (5.6km)	1½ hrs	26ft (8m)
Tealby and Kirmond le Mire	81	Tealby	TF 158908	7¼ miles (11.7km)	3½ hrs	482ft (147m)
Tennyson Country	26	Tetford	TF 333748	5 miles (8km)	2½ hrs	295ft (90m)
Thornton Abbey	18	Thornton Abbey	TA 114189	3½ miles (5.6km)	1½ hrs	42ft (13m)
Top of the Wolds	78	Caistor	TA 118 014	8 miles (12.9km)	3½ hrs	492ft (150m)
Vale of Belvoir	42	Woolsthorpe by Belvoir	SK 837341	6½ miles (10.5km)	3 hrs	338ft (103m)
Walesby, Claxby and Normanby le Wold	62	Walesby	TF 133924	5¼ miles (8.4km)	2½ hrs	479ft (146m)
Woodhall Spa	47	Woodhall Spa	TF 192630	6½ miles (10.5km)	3 hrs	56ft (17m)

Comments

The walk starts by a picturesque mill and two adjacent churches and includes an attractive stretch beside the Louth Canal and fine views across reclaimed marshland.

The walk takes you across the countryside of the Bain valley near Horncastle, with an attractive and relaxing finale alongside the Horncastle Canal.

The open and sweeping views extend to Humberside on this fine walk in the northern wolds, which passes through two hamlets with medieval churches.

This varied walk starts by the Humber Bridge and includes a Saxon church, view of The Wolds and attractive walking beside the Humber Estuary.

Three waterways – Maud Foster Drain, Frith Bank Drain and the River Witham – are used on this Fenland walk to the north of Boston. There are particularly memorable views of Boston Stump.

There is pleasant woodland walking with superb views over the valley of the East Glen River.

An opening walk across fields and reclaimed coastal marshes is followed by a final stretch along a sandy beach.

The route through pleasant wolds country passes a watermill, now a wildfowl garden, and takes you through the lovely, steep-sided Swaby valley.

The walk follows a lengthy stretch of the River Welland to the north of Crowland across a totally flat Fenland landscape.

The first part of the walk is above the Bain valley; the final stretch is beside the river. The views are superb throughout, even extending to Lincoln Cathedral.

There are superb views on this walk, the first half of which is mostly along the base of Lincoln Edge. The return is along the top, passing through four limestone villages.

This route explores the fringe of the RSPB's largest reserve in Lincolnshire, following embankments beside The Wash and through the fertile, reclaimed marshland of the Fens.

This walk is an easy introduction to the exhilarating, limitless horizons of The Wash and the complex sea defences of the area. Coasters and bombers add interest!

This pleasant walk in the flat country of the Isle of Axholme starts in the attractive village where John and Charles Wesley were born.

Three attractive villages are linked on this outstanding walk in the northern wolds, not far from Grimsby and the Humber Estuary.

Some of Lincoln's major historic sites are combined with a walk alongside the Fossdyke, originally cut by the Romans.

There are wide views across the Trent valley from Lincoln Edge at the start and end of the walk.

The walk links the historic town of Stamford with two attractive villages. There are fine views and beautiful riverside meadows.

This walk in the Witham valley includes two villages, woodland, monastic remains and a series of wide views.

The walk links the historic town of Stamford with two attractive villages. There are fine views and beautiful riverside meadows.

This short walk is full of interest – two medieval churches, a castle, the Battle of Britain display and attractive walking beside the River Bain.

A walk across a typically rolling wolds landscape of gentle slopes and wide dry valleys, starting in an outstandingly attractive village.

This attractive walk in the heart of the Lincolnshire Wolds passes through the tiny hamlet where the great Victorian poet was born and lived for much of his early life.

On this circuit of the country around Thornton Abbey there are many views of the striking abbey ruins.

From the small market town of Caistor, the walk rises through peaceful, green valleys in the North Wolds to Lincolnshire's highest ridge, with excellent views all round.

Main features of the walk are the wide vistas over the vale, attractive walking beside the Grantham Canal and the magnificent views of Belvoir Castle, seen from many different angles.

This is a classic walk over some of the highest and most scenic parts of the Lincolnshire Wolds, with the chance to visit the Ramblers' Church above Walesby.

An opening stretch across fields and along quiet lanes is followed by a delightful finale through some of the woodlands around Woodhall Spa.

Introduction to Lincolnshire and the Wolds

Lincolnshire is one of England's largest counties, second in size only to Yorkshire. Like Yorkshire it was traditionally divided into three areas: Lindsey in the north, Kesteven in the south-west and Holland in the south-east.

The usual response when telling someone that you are going to Lincolnshire is a dismissive comment about its flatness. A brief glance at some of the photographs in this guide will confirm that there is a lot more to the county. It does have hills that rise to over 540ft (165m) – but the belief that it mainly consists of flat landscapes is the commonest misconception. Just try walking up Steep Hill in Lincoln to the cathedral and castle and never again will you believe that Lincolnshire is flat.

Two main upland areas

In reality Lincolnshire comprises a lot of flat country broken up by two main upland areas, one long and narrow and the other shorter but wider. Perhaps the easiest way in which to understand its topography is to take an imaginary journey across it from west to east.

The western part of Lincolnshire is flat, extending from the Humber estuary in the north, through the Isle of Axholme and the Trent valley to the wide expanses of the Vale of Belvoir in the south.

Looking eastward, the western escarpment of Lincoln Edge (or Lincoln Cliff) is seen on the horizon, not a steep escarpment for the most part but nevertheless a significant physical feature. This is a long but narrow limestone ridge, part of the range of limestone uplands that extend north-eastwards across England from the Cotswolds, through south Warwickshire, Northamptonshire, Rutland and Lincolnshire, and on into Yorkshire. Here there are attractive old towns and villages built from the local stone, whose colouring varies from pale cream in some areas to darker orangey-brown ironstone at both the north and south ends. It is this ironstone that gave rise to the iron and steel industries of Scunthorpe in the north and Corby – just over the Northamptonshire border – in the south. Lincoln grew up where the River Witham cuts through this limestone ridge, and the towers of its hilltop cathedral dominate the city and much of the surrounding countryside, visible from over 20 miles (32km) away.

The Wolds – rolling countryside at its finest

To the east of Lincoln Edge stretches the clay vale of Lincoln Heath and beyond that are the Lincolnshire Wolds, the highest hills and arguably the most attractive countryside in the county. The Wolds are chalk hills, part of the series of chalk outcrops that extends roughly north-eastwards from the Chilterns, appearing at intervals in Cambridgeshire, continuing through Lincolnshire and reappearing on the other side of the Humber as the Yorkshire Wolds. This is rolling countryside at its finest, with slopes that range from gentle to moderately steep, wide dry valleys and panoramic views from the higher points over heath, marsh and fen. Among the many delightful villages scattered throughout the wolds is the tiny hamlet of Somersby, where Alfred Lord Tennyson was born, the son of the village rector.

The coast

Lastly on this west–east journey across the county there is the coastal strip running from the Humber to the Wash, partly reclaimed marshland and constantly vulnerable to the threat of invasion by the sea. It is a flat and fairly uniform coastline with virtually no cliffs, no estuaries and consequently no harbours between Grimsby on the Humber and Boston on the Wash. It is also a coastline of wide, sandy beaches – if inclined to be bracing as the legendary advertisement for Skegness states – and in the Victorian era, a string of holiday resorts grew up when rail links were created with the nearby industrial areas of Yorkshire and the East Midlands. A trip to Cleethorpes, Mablethorpe or 'Skeggy' became part of a way of life for many people in these areas, until at least the 1960s.

One area remains which does not fit into this west-east pattern but which no guide to the county can ignore. Most of south and south-east Lincolnshire comprises the vast, seemingly limitless expanses of the Fens, which extend across the county borders into neighbouring Cambridgeshire and Norfolk. Contrary to what some people say, these fenlands – and indeed the coastal marshlands, Isle of Axholme and the other flat landscapes of Lincolnshire – are not boring or featureless but have a unique appeal and a strange, haunting beauty. Wide skies, endless vistas, a sense of space and – certainly on the marshlands around the Wash – a feeling of remoteness and isolation can be experienced nowhere else in the region.

Lincoln

Lincoln is the focal point of the county and has been so since Roman times. The Romans built a town here – Lindum Colonia – where the River Witham turns abruptly eastwards and cuts through the limestone ridge of Lincoln Edge to flow on to the sea. They also constructed the Fossdyke to link Lincoln to the Trent, still in existence and probably the earliest canal in the country. A few Roman remains survive in the city, notably the Newport Arch, one of only two surviving Roman gateways in England.

About 1,000 years after the Romans, the Norman conquerors built a

The Saxon church at Barton-upon-Humber

castle and moved the seat of the diocese here. Both castle and cathedral are built on the site of the Roman fort and face each other on the highest part of the ridge. Lincoln Cathedral, a masterpiece of Gothic architecture, is regarded as one of the finest churches in Europe. Nearby are the ruins of the palace of the powerful medieval bishops, and on the steep downhill walk to the lower town you pass two of the earliest domestic buildings in the country – both dating from the 12th century. Spanning the Witham is the High Bridge, one of the few in England that still has buildings on it.

Stamford, Spalding and Boston
Lincolnshire has other historic towns, all well worth exploring. Stamford is a most appealing town, with a wealth of late-medieval churches and handsome houses, built from the local limestone. It is situated at the far south-western tip of the county, scarcely ½ mile (800m) from the borders of no less than three other counties – Cambridgeshire, Northamptonshire and Rutland. The views of its towers and spires from the water meadows adjoining the River Welland are particularly memorable.

Downstream along the Welland, Spalding is equally attractive but in a different way. This is a fenland town, with brick-built houses lining the river. It is the bulb capital of England and in springtime the town is a riot of colour.

Boston, situated at the mouth of the Witham, was once one of the most important ports in the country, and the great medieval church, noted for its strikingly tall tower, Boston Stump, is a reflection of its medieval prosperity. It was Puritans who emigrated from here to the New World in the 17th century who founded the town of Boston, Massachusetts.

Prayer and Pestilence
The magnificence of Lincolnshire's churches equals those of the more famous Norfolk and Cotswold 'wool churches'. The churches of major towns such as Louth, Grantham and Boston resulted from the wealth generated by England's 'white gold' – Boston was second only to London

as England's principal wool port: The Wolds were, in medieval times, vast sheep ranches. Village churches, often of the golden ironstone or distinctive greenstone that typify much of the county, reflected this wealth and were mostly paid for by lords of the manor who made fortunes from the wool trade.

The Cistercian monks, who were granted huge estates, were equally pious but less magnanimous to the peasant population; the huge number of deserted villages in Lincolnshire results partly from the Black Death in the 14th century, but also from the deliberate depopulation of entire districts by the seclusion-seeking canons, who destroyed villages but left churches intact. The county's marvellous array of isolated medieval churches owes much to this misanthropic community, who literally became wealthy off the backs of sheep and who unwittingly acted as early preservers of an ancient heritage.

Walking Lincolnshire

What Lincolnshire lacks in altitude (its highest point is just 551ft [168m]), it more than makes up for in the sheer variety of walking opportunities and landscapes. The contrasts between The Wolds, the coastal and vale plains and the Fens are striking; all are laced by public rights of way, the waymarking of which is exemplary and the maintenance of such first class. As a relatively undiscovered walking destination, its paths remain refreshingly peaceful, the province of locals and discerning ramblers.

The walks in this *Pathfinder* guide offer a taste of this kaleidoscope of countryside and seek to introduce the curious visitor to a memorable diversity of built and natural landscapes in this relatively little-known part of Britain.

With the introduction of **'gps enabled' walks,** you will see that this book now includes a list of waypoints alongside the description of the walk. We have included these so that you can enjoy the full benefits of gps should you wish to. Gps is an amazingly useful and entertaining navigational aid, and you do not need to be computer literate to enjoy it.

GPS waypoint co-ordinates add value to your walk. You will now have the extra advantage of introducing 'direction' into your walking which will enhance your leisure walking and make it safer. Use of a gps brings greater confidence and security and you will find you cover ground a lot faster should you need to.

For more detailed information on using your gps, a *Pathfinder Guide* introducing you to gps and digital mapping is now available. *GPS for Walkers*, written by experienced gps teacher and navigation trainer Clive Thomas, is available in bookshops (ISBN 978-0-7117-4445-5) or order online at www.totalwalking.co.uk

Introduction

Alvingham and the Louth Canal

Start	Church Lane, Alvingham		**GPS waypoints**
Distance	3½ miles (5.6km)		✐ TF 366 913
Approximate time	1½ hours		Ⓐ TF 368 912
			Ⓑ TF 375 922
Parking	Lay-by near Alvingham Mill, marked 'Two Churches'		Ⓒ TF 385 909
			Ⓓ TF 375 907
Refreshments	None		
Ordnance Survey maps	Explorer 283 (Louth & Mablethorpe), Landranger 113 (Grimsby, Louth & Market Rasen)		

The walk starts by a picturesque watermill and passes through a churchyard that contains two churches to reach the banks of the Louth Canal. It continues by the canal before heading off across reclaimed marshland to the village of North Cockerington and on to the start. The stretch beside the canal is most attractive, and there are immense views over the marshes, especially looking towards the coast.

The picturesque 18th century Alvingham Mill (private) is on a site dating back over 900 years; it is the sole survivor of 13 mills that the tiny River Lud once powered.

✐ From the parking area, cross the flat bridge and go ahead through the concreted farmyard to a hand-gate into

Alvingham Mill

the churchyard. Turn right on the path that brushes the tower of one of two churches here. This nearer, smaller one – St Mary's, now redundant – served the parish of North Cockerington; the adjacent one – St Adelwold's – still serves as Alvingham's parish church. St Mary's may have been a chapel belonging to a long-gone local abbey.

Ⓐ Cross a footbridge over a brook; then a longer one over the Louth Canal and turn left along the embankment. The navigation linked Louth to the sea and was abandoned in 1929; moves are afoot to reopen it. The path uses two stiles before a kissing-gate leads into a tarred lane at High Bridge. Ⓑ Turn right and walk to the end at a T-junction. Here turn right on an enclosed track; at a fork near a cottage keep left, cross a flat bridge and walk the field track beside a drain. This winds

The Louth Canal at Alvingham

across the reclaimed marshland, now rich farmland, to reach a lane.

Keep ahead for ¹/₂ mile (800m) to round a right-bend. As the lane then bends left, take the stile on the right **C** to join a path above Green Dike. Follow

this through to another lane, along which turn right.

Shortly, turn left **D** along Meadow Lane and walk through North Cockerington. Just past the telephone box and Barn Owl Cottage, turn right along a track, Church Walk, and trace this to a lane. Cross straight over to join a wide green way that leads back to the footbridges at **A**. Cross these and walk back to the start. ●

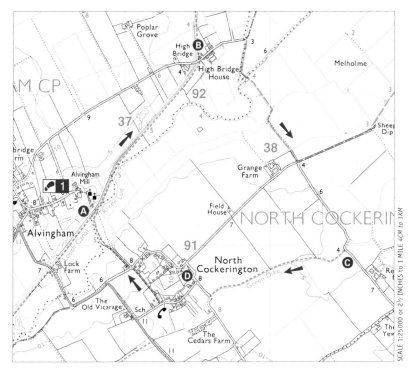

Tattershall and Coningsby

		GPS waypoints
Start	Tattershall	🖉 TF 212 579
Distance	3½ miles (5.6km)	Ⓐ TF 213 577
Approximate time	1½ hours	Ⓑ TF 221 578
Parking	Off Tattershall Market Place; free	Ⓒ TF 226 583
Refreshments	Shops, pubs and cafés in Tattershall and Coningsby	Ⓓ TF 228 586
Ordnance Survey maps	Explorer 261 (Boston), Landranger 122 (Skegness & Horncastle)	

Although a short and flat walk, the considerable historic interest ranges from a redbrick 15th-century castle and two medieval churches to a Battle of Britain display. There is also pleasant walking beside the River Bain.

Tattershall is dominated by its castle and church, which rise majestically above the flat landscape. Both were built in the 15th century by Ralph, third Lord Cromwell, who was Lord High Treasurer of England during the reign of Henry VI and one of the most powerful men in the country.

The dark, redbrick castle is a tall, four-storied tower-house, which replaced a more modest earlier structure. After falling into disrepair, it was restored by Lord Curzon at the

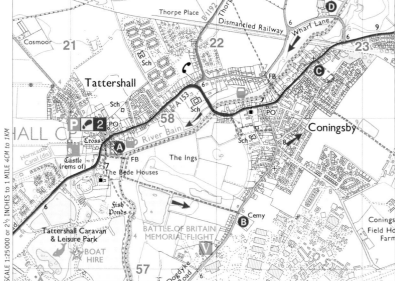

Tattershall and the River Bain

beginning of the 20th century and is now maintained by the National Trust. The collegiate church, a superb example of the Perpendicular style, is unusual in that it has transepts but no central tower, though it does have an imposing west tower. The spacious interior is of almost cathedral-like proportions.

🖌 From the car park, walk across the Market Place to the main road and turn right towards Sleaford, the castle and church. Immediately cross to the left and take the signposted footpath along an enclosed tarred path. Cross a footbridge over the disused Horncastle Canal, turn left beside it and walk to and across a bridge over the River Bain.

🅐 Turn right along the bank; in 100 yds (91m) turn left on a wide path which shortly passes to the left of a lake and continues as a raised track through to a road 🅑. Turn right for about ¼ mile (400m) if you wish to visit the Battle of Britain Memorial Flight, where there are Second World War aircraft and a visitor centre with displays and exhibits of the battle.

The route continues to the left into Coningsby. At a road junction, bear slightly left along Silver Street, then turn right into Park Lane and follow the road around a left-hand bend to a T-junction 🅒. Turn right, turn left along Wharf Lane (signposted to Tattershall Thorpe and Woodhall Spa) and immediately after crossing a bridge over the River Bain, turn left to climb a stile 🅓. Now follows a delightful part of the route as you continue across riverside meadows and over several stiles, with fine views ahead of the tower of Coningsby's medieval church, noted for the huge clock on the west tower.

Cross a tarmac path to the right of a footbridge, use the kissing-gate opposite and continue by the river to reach another kissing-gate onto a road. Turn left, cross the bridge, turn right through a further kissing-gate and continue along the other bank of the Bain to a footbridge 🅐. Here you rejoin the outward route and turn right over the bridge to retrace your steps to the starting point. ●

Thornton Abbey

		GPS waypoints
Start	Thornton Abbey	✔ TA 114 189
Distance	3½ miles (5.6km)	Ⓐ TA 122 191
Approximate time	1½ hours	Ⓑ TA 126 179
Parking	Thornton Abbey car park; free	Ⓒ TA 114 174
Refreshments	None	Ⓓ TA 109 188
Ordnance Survey maps	Explorer 284 (Grimsby, Cleethorpes & Immingham), Landranger 113 (Grimsby, Louth & Market Rasen)	

The walk is almost a perfect square, and its chief focal point, the imposing gatehouse of Thornton Abbey, is in sight for most of the way amidst the flat terrain. The views are particularly impressive on the last stretch between Thornton Abbey station and the start. Although this is a quiet walk with a genuinely remote feel, glimpses of the oil refineries of Humberside on the horizon are a reminder that the 21st century is not far away.

Thornton Abbey was founded as an Augustinian priory in 1139, raised to abbey status in 1148 and suppressed by Henry VIII in 1539. Little survives of the church and monastic buildings, except for part of the chapter-house, but the brick and stone gatehouse is one of the largest and most elaborate in the country. Built in the late 14th century, it was partly fortified, and the approach is lined with redbrick arcaded walling.

🏃 Facing the abbey gatehouse, turn left to the road and bear right along it. At a public footpath sign, turn right through a kissing-gate, keep ahead to cross a footbridge over a drain, climb

Ruins of Thornton Abbey

steps and continue along the right-hand edge of a field. After going through a kissing-gate, the easiest route would be to continue straight ahead but the line of the right of way is to bear right to keep by a line of trees on the right and follow the curve of the field edge to the left to go through another kissing-gate.

Turn right to cross a footbridge and bear slightly left across the field to cross another footbridge over East Halton Beck. Walk ahead across the field, keeping some paces left of the lake to find a stile and old gate in the field corner, rising then to join a road. Turn right; in 300 yds (274m) turn right through a gateway to join a fieldside track **A**. This track skirts the left edge of fields and, in the corner of the last field, follow the track first to the right and then turn left through a gate. Walk along an enclosed track, which later continues across a field, rising gently to go through a gate onto a lane **B**.

Turn right along the winding lane to a T-junction, turn left (in the Ulceby direction) and, just after a right-hand bend, go over a level-crossing and immediately turn right along a track **C**. The track curves left to enter a field and, at a waymarked post, turn right along its right-hand edge. Keep in a straight line along the right-hand edge of a series of fields, parallel to the rail line and with a drain below on the right. Where the drain ends, follow the field edge as it bends first right and then left and continue to a road by Thornton Abbey station.

Do not turn left to the road but turn right through a hand-gate **D**, recross the railway lines at the near-end of the platforms and use another hand-gate. With a magnificent view of the abbey gatehouse ahead, follow a grassy track back to the start.

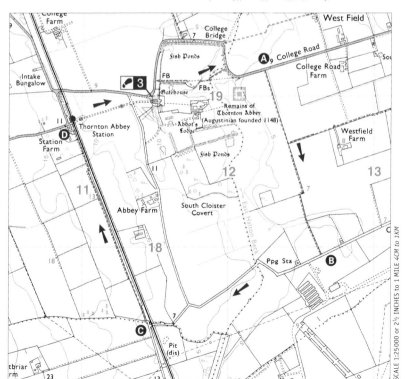

Guy's Head

Start	Guy's Head	GPS waypoints
Distance	3¾ miles (6km)	TF 491 256
Approximate time	2 hours	Ⓐ TF 482 279
Parking	Lay-by near the old lighthouse; free	Ⓑ TF 477 281
		Ⓒ TF 482 268
Refreshments	None on walk; two pubs in Gedney Drove End	
Ordnance Survey maps	Explorer 249 (Spalding and Holbeach), Landranger 131 (Boston & Spalding)	

Here is an easy introduction to the unique landscapes of The Wash. The typical endless skies, sea-marshes, sandbanks and mudflats beside the area's rivers are an artist's and birdwatcher's paradise – binoculars are a must! Wildflowers include sea asters, and the locally popular delicacy of samphire is harvested nearby at Gedney Drove End. The occasional explosion comes courtesy of the RAF bombing range offshore here.

The two modest lighthouses, 'The Twins' – one on the Lincolnshire side, the other on the Norfolk side – mark the mouth of the tidal navigation of the River Nene, which is still used by sizeable coasters. Both buildings are now private residences; the one on the far bank was home to the conservationist and artist Sir Peter Scott.

Take the narrow, waymarked path between the embankment wall and the lighthouse's garden, use the stile/gate and walk out onto the embankment, heading towards the limitless horizon of The Wash. Climb a stile, cross above the sluices, use another stile and continue along the bank, which shortly curves left. This area is part of the largest National Nature Reserve in England, conserving the saltmarsh, sand and mudflats upon which countless resident and transient wildfowl rely. Seals are also dependent on the flats and sandbanks – with luck

and powerful binoculars you may just see some at low water on the island just offshore or hauled out on the glistening mud.

Far out in The Wash, the old hulks visible are targets for the offshore bombing range here; a monitoring tower is visible in the distance, much farther along the sea bank. Upon reaching a gate and stile Ⓐ, leave the main embankment and follow the track as it curves inland to reach a lane. Turn left along it Ⓑ and walk for 200 yds (183m) or so to a waymarked path on the left; take this and join the line of an earlier sea bank, built about a century ago. At a corner, climb the old steps on your right to continue along this old defence, eventually reaching a junction with a lane Ⓒ. Go straight ahead here to return to the parking area.

0	200	400	600	800 METRES	1	
						KILOMETRES
						MILES
0	200	400	600 YARDS	½		

The Nene Twins

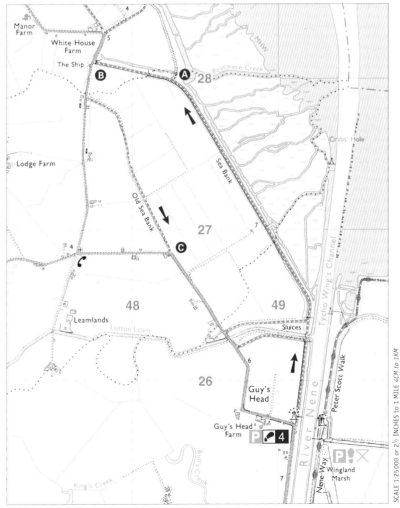

North Carlton and Scampton

		GPS waypoints
Start	Till Bridge Lane Viewpoint, at junction of A1500 and B1398	✐ SK 954 783
Distance	4½ miles (7.2km)	Ⓐ SK 950 776
Approximate time	2 hours	Ⓑ SK 939 775
Parking	Car park at start; free	Ⓒ SK 934 788
Refreshments	Pub at Scampton	Ⓓ SK 938 787
Ordnance Survey maps	Explorer 272 (Lincoln), Landranger 121 (Lincoln & Newark-on-Trent)	Ⓔ SK 948 788
		Ⓕ SK 950 792
		Ⓖ SK 950 783

From the starting point on Lincoln Edge, views across the Trent Valley are extensive. Along the way, the walk visits the sedate villages of North Carlton and Scampton. Above the latter is RAF Scampton, home to the Red Arrows and from where the 617 'Dambusters' squadron flew 'Operation Chastise' against the Ruhr dams in 1943.

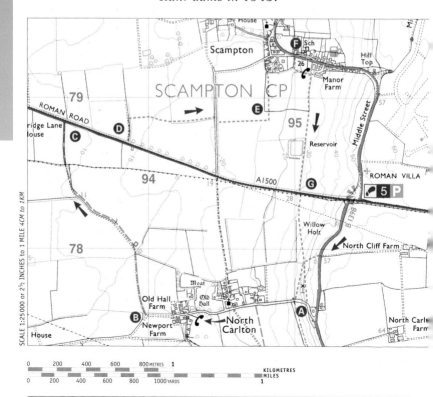

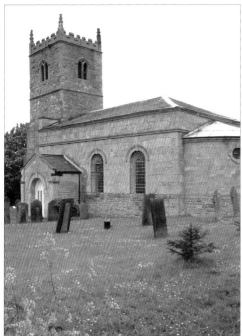

North Carlton church

Start by walking along the B1398 (signposted to Burton and Lincoln) and, after ¼ mile (400m), turn right at a public footpath sign and head downhill across a field, veering left and making for a hedge corner. Turn left and continue across the field, keeping roughly in line with telegraph poles and, on the far side, go through a hedge gap onto a lane.

Ⓐ Turn right and follow the lane through the hamlet of North Carlton, passing to the left of the church. This is a mainly Georgian building, rare for a small village church, with a 15th-century tower. Where the lane curves left, turn right Ⓑ along a tarred track at a public bridleway sign. Bend left in front of the barns (ignore the misleading 'No footpath' sign) and trace the rougher field road for ¼ mile (400m) to the point where it curves away to the left. Here, fork ahead right on a grassy track, following this beside a hedge (right) to reach the main road. Ⓒ Turn right and cross carefully.

In ¼ mile (400m) take the waymarked track on the left Ⓓ along the right edge of a field. In 150 yds (137m) turn right through a waymarked hedge gap, cross the flat bridge and head straight across the field, in-line with the radar tower at Scampton airbase. Go through another hedge gap and drift slightly left to use a gap to access a lane. Turn right and then immediately left along a track to reach a T-junction. Ⓔ Turn left alongside the old hedge and follow this grassy path through to a lane at the edge of Scampton.

Turn right to the nearby junction; here turn left and walk through to the village church. St John's churchyard holds many poignant memorial stones to British and Commonwealth aircrew who did not return to the base, and to the crew of a German bomber that crashed nearby. Turn right from the churchyard gate along the main road, which sweeps left into the village. The village pub – The Dambusters Inn – is at the far end of the main street; the route of the walk is along the waymarked footpath on the right Ⓕ immediately after the lane joins from the right, opposite the dormer bungalow 'Stonecroft'.

Walk the right edge of the field to the corner; turn left here and then right in front of the barns along a field road. The track passes between reservoir embankments and at one point jinks right across a ditch as waymarked. Upon reaching the main road Ⓖ turn left to return to the start.

Barton and the River Humber

		GPS waypoints
Start	Barton-upon-Humber, Humber Bridge Viewing Area	✏ TA 027 233
Distance	5½ miles (8.9km)	Ⓐ TA 028 229
Approximate time	2½ hours	Ⓑ TA 034 219
Parking	Clay Pits car park, Waterside Road; free	Ⓒ TA 017 221
		Ⓓ TA 014 228
Refreshments	All services in Barton-upon-Humber	Ⓔ TA 005 230
Ordnance Survey maps	Explorer 281 (Ancholme Valley), Landranger 112 (Scunthorpe)	

The wide-ranging views on this walk include the northern slopes of the Lincolnshire Wolds, up and down the Humber Estuary and across the river to the southern edge of the Yorkshire Wolds, and, of course, stunning views of the Humber Bridge near where the walk begins. The route takes you through the small town of Barton-upon-Humber, passing its celebrated Saxon church, before heading across fields for a final 1½ mile (2.4km) stretch beside the estuary.

Barton Clay Pits and the adjoining Far Ings Nature Reserve comprise a series of flooded clay pits along the south bank of the Humber Estuary, dug for the making of tiles and bricks. They are now a haven for wildlife. The starting point is an excellent place from which to appreciate the beauty and elegance of the Humber Bridge, opened in 1981 and one of the suspension bridges with the longest spans in the world. The length of the main span is 4,626ft (1,410m).

✏ Start by facing the river, turn left and, at the

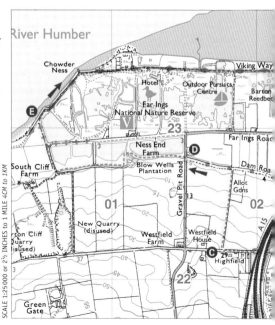

SCALE 1:25000 or 2½ INCHES to 1 MILE 4CM to 1KM

far end of the car park, take a path through trees. Turn left at a T-junction in front of a pool, walk along a straight path to a road, turn left and, at a T-junction **Ⓐ**, turn right into Barton-upon-Humber. Pass the station to reach a junction of roads and continue along the narrow street ahead (Fleetgate), passing to the right of the White Swan. Take the second street on the left (High Street), bear left at a junction to continue along High Street and then Burgate, walk past St Mary's Church and, at a T-junction, take the tarmac path opposite to the Saxon church of St Peter **Ⓑ**.

The close proximity of two outstanding medieval churches is an indication that Barton was a prosperous town and important Humber port, until eclipsed from the late 13th century onwards by the rise of Hull on the opposite side of the river. St Mary's, which dates from the 12th century – with later additions –

is a large and impressive town church but major interest is inevitably centred on St Peter's for its Saxon architecture. The west end and tower remain of the original 10th-century church; the rest was rebuilt and added to over the following centuries.

Retrace your steps along Burgate and High Street and, at the junction, do not follow your earlier route by continuing to the right along High Street but bear slightly left, along Hungate to a cross-roads. Turn right and, where the main road bends right, keep ahead along Westfield Road. At the end of the road, keep ahead along a tarmac track to pass under the A15, climb steps and continue along a narrow lane. At a public footpath fingerpost just past Westfield Lodge, turn right **Ⓒ** on to a path that heads gently downhill along the left-hand edge of a field. Ahead are magnificent views of the Humber Bridge and the estuary, with the southern slopes of the Yorkshire Wolds on the horizon.

Continue along the right-hand edge of the next field, in the corner turn left and turn right to cross a footbridge over a drain on to a narrow lane. Turn left to a T-junction **Ⓓ**, and cross straight over the lane to join an enclosed path between a drain and a lake. Cross a wide footbridge and then swing left along a fenced path signed for South Ferriby, skirting the edge of wildfowl lakes to reach a hedge gap in the distant corner, here climbing onto a rough lane. Turn right along this signed byway and walk through to the estuaryside embankment.

Ⓔ Go through the kissing-gate on your right and simply follow this bank-top path between the Humber Estuary and the Far Ings Nature Reserve. About $^1/_4$ mile (400m) after passing beneath the suspension bridge, turn right down steps to return to the start. ●

Tennyson Country

Start	Tetford	**GPS waypoints**	
Distance	5 miles (8km)	 TF 333 748	
Approximate time	2½ hours	**A** TF 349 744	
		B TF 351 742	
Parking	Roadside parking near Tetford church; free	**C** TF 353 737	
		D TF 343 726	
Refreshments	Pub in Tetford	**E** TF 333 732	
Ordnance Survey maps	Explorer 273 (Lincolnshire Wolds South), Landranger 122 (Skegness & Horncastle)		

The first part of this route in the heart of 'Tennyson Country' is along the line of a Roman road to the east of the village of Tetford. It continues over the wolds, dropping into the tiny hamlet of Somersby, where Tennyson was born and brought up. From here, lanes, tracks and field paths lead back to the start. There are fine views over the wolds from the higher points on the walk.

Start by the mainly 15th-century greenstone church and walk along the narrow lane to the left of it. At the corner in 75 yds (68m) use the kissing-gate into the churchyard and walk through to a stile over the boundary wall. Head slightly right, shortly passing through the first of a number of threadbare old hedge lines, tracing the course of a Roman road that ran from Lincoln to Burgh le Marsh. If you pass a footbridge on your left, you are too near the edge of the field. The walk keeps along the left edge of a line of trees, passes a tall ash and crosses a field to reach a stile about 120 yds (110m) in from the left field corner.

Climb the stile and bear slightly right across the next field to cross a footbridge. Walk along the right-hand edge of a field, cross a footbridge, keep along the left-hand edge of the next field, cross a footbridge in the corner and go through a kissing-gate. Head across a field corner to go through another kissing-gate, cross another footbridge, continue across the next field, cross a footbridge and keep ahead to a footpath post. Cross a track, continue across a field, cross a footbridge on the far side, turn right **A** along the right-hand edge of a field and cross one more footbridge onto a lane.

Turn left and, at a public bridleway sign, turn right **B** along an enclosed uphill path, which passes along the right-hand edge of Willow Bank Wood at the top. From here there are superb

Descending to Somersby

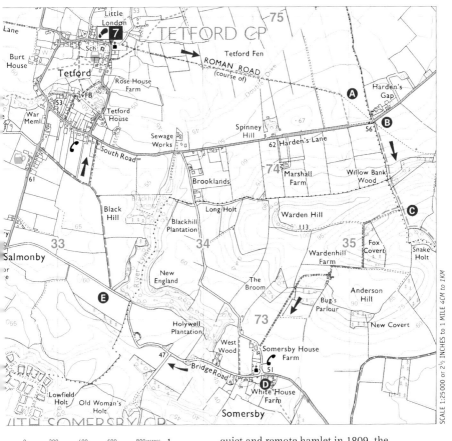

SCALE 1:25000 or 2½ INCHES to 1 MILE *4CM to 1KM*

```
0    200   400   600   800 METRES  1
                                   KILOMETRES
                                   MILES
0    200   400   600 YARDS   ½
```

views over the wolds. The path descends but, after about 200 yds (183m), turn right **C** at a fingerpost, pass through a wide gap in the hedge and walk alongside a fence on your left to a T-junction just past a neck of woodland. Turn left along a track down into a dip and up again to another T-junction, turn right, and the track bends left to Wardenhill Farm. Follow the track to the right in front of the farm buildings and the track later curves left and heads downhill – a grand view ahead over the wolds here – to Somersby House Farm.

In front of the farm, turn left along a lane to a T-junction **D** and turn right, passing to the left of Somersby church. Alfred, Lord Tennyson was born in this

quiet and remote hamlet in 1809, the son of the rector, and lived here for most of his early life. His birthplace is a private residence and not open to the public. The small, plain greenstone church has a display about the poet and his life in this part of Lincolnshire.

Continue along the lane, following it around right and left-hand bends. After almost one mile (1.6km), turn right **E** at a public bridleway sign, along a track by the left-hand edge of a field. The track narrows to a path that bears slightly left and becomes enclosed. At a footpath post, turn right along the left-hand edge of a field, in the corner continue along an enclosed, tree-lined path and climb a stile onto a road. Turn left and take the first road on the right (East Road), which leads back to the starting point. ●

Claythorpe Mill
and the Swaby valley

Start	Aby Village Hall
Distance	5½ miles (8.9km)
Approximate time	2½ hours
Parking	Roadside near Aby Village Hall and school; free
Refreshments	The Vine Inn, South Thoresby is just off the route. Refreshments (for paying visitors) at Claythorpe Mill
Ordnance Survey maps	Explorer 274 (Skegness, Alford & Spilsby), Landranger 122 (Skegness & Horncastle)

GPS waypoints

🖉	TF 412 783
Ⓐ	TF 413 783
Ⓑ	TF 415 790
Ⓒ	TF 411 791
Ⓓ	TF 398 785
Ⓔ	TF 388 776
Ⓕ	TF 395 775
Ⓖ	TF 401 770
Ⓗ	TF 406 775
Ⓙ	TF 413 775

This walk on the eastern fringes of the wolds links four quiet hamlets and passes a picturesque watermill. From Aby you head across fields to Claythorpe Mill and then on through the wide valley of the Great Eau to Belleau. The route continues to the edge of Swaby, and this is followed by a delightful ramble through the beautiful and steep-sided Swaby valley and on to South Thoresby. A combination of field paths, lanes and tracks leads back to the start.

🖉 The walk starts on the 'No Through Road' in Aby village centre. Walk past the school on your left and turn left in a further 100 yds (91m) Ⓐ at a fingerpost pointing the way as along the tarred driveway past Paddock House. Climb stiles either side of the stable yard and turn left on the enclosed path that circuits a paddock. Use another stile, cross a plank bridge and walk the right-hand edge of the field to a fingerpost at an offset corner. From here head half-right, aiming for the distant old railway arch visible over the crest of the field.

Join the lane here and walk beneath the arch to a nearby junction. Ⓑ Turn left along the lane signed for Claythorpe Mill. This imposing, white-painted building on the river Great Eau no longer operates as a corn mill but is now the base for a wildlife and wildfowl sanctuary and visitor centre, open daily from March to October. Pass by the mill and wind up the lane, shortly keeping left at a fork. On your left is the goods shed of the old railway, the former Louth to Firsby line. Just before the lane bends to the right, turn left at a footpath fingerpost Ⓒ, cross a cattle-grid and bend right on the field road, walking through to a stile immediately to the right of the cottage. Climb the stile and turn left to a crossing of paths at the far edge of the cottage's garden. Here continue ahead, turn right along the nearby field edge (a deep drain on your left) and walk to and across a footbridge, then take a straight path towards the distant buildings at Belleau hamlet. At a lane, turn left to reach the settlement.

Head gently uphill, bending right to pass the Victorian church, and continue to a T-junction. Turn right and, at a public footpath sign, turn left **D** along the left-hand edge of a field, by woodland on the left. At the corner of the wood, keep straight ahead across the field, passing to the right of a small clump of trees, and continue to a hedge gap on the far side. Go through, keep ahead across the next field – the houses of Swaby are seen below – and on the far side, continue along the right-hand edge of woodland. Look out for where you climb a waymarked stile, head downhill along a tree-lined path and

climb another stile onto a tarmac track on the edge of Swaby **E**. Turn left and, where the track ends, bear left at a public bridleway sign to South Thoresby, along a grassy track above a pool to a stile. After climbing it, the route continues beside Swaby Beck through the lovely Swaby valley. Go through a gate, keep ahead through the valley, ignore a permissive footpath sign on the right but, at the next footpath post **F**, bear right through scrub and trees to enter a field.

Walk along the right-hand edge of the field and look out for a yellow-waymarked post that directs you to turn right through another area of trees and scrub. Cross a footbridge, keep ahead

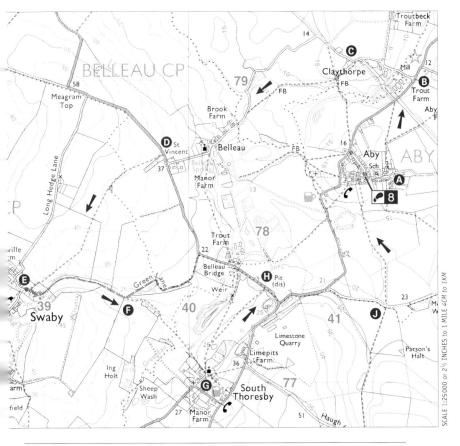

along boardwalks to a public footpath sign and turn left. Head across a field, veering right away from its left-hand edge, walk along more boardwalks and continue to a footbridge over the Great Eau on the far side. Cross it and keep ahead along the right-hand edge of the next field to a stile in the corner **G**.

Do not climb the stile if continuing along the route but *do so if you wish to visit the church and pub at South Thoresby. The church is immediately to the left, a small brick Georgian building dating from the 1730s. For the pub, keep along a tarmac track, which curves right to a road, and turn left.*

To continue with the route, turn sharp left in front of the stile, initially along the right-hand edge of the field and then across pasture as the estate wall peels away. Favour your right hand, looking to climb a stile over a fence just a few yards away from where the brick wall ends. Keep ahead on the grassy track across the abandoned field, eventually reaching a lane. **H** Turn right and walk through to the nearby T-junction. Turn left and walk around the bend to the next junction; here fork right along the lane signed for Greenfield and Aldford and, at a public footpath sign, turn left **J** and head across a field, making for a waymarked post just left of a tree.

From this point head slightly left, aiming for the left-hand end of the distant housing to a fingerpost at a hedged corner. Keep ahead to a nearby fingerpost; here turn right beside a drain to reach a footbridge, cross this and go ahead across the field to join an enclosed path leading to a village lane in Aby. Turn right to return to the start. ●

Footbridge across the Great Eau

Stamford, Easton on the Hill and Tinwell

		GPS waypoints
Start	Stamford, Red Lion Square	
Distance	5½ miles (8.9km)	TF 029 070
Approximate time	2½ hours	**A** TF 027 067
Parking	Stamford; Pay and Display	**B** TF 019 060
Refreshments	All facilities in Stamford, pub and shop in Easton on the Hill	**C** TF 011 047
		D TF 011 042
Ordnance Survey maps	Explorer 234 (Rutland Water), Landranger 141 (Kettering & Corby)	**E** TF 008 061

This is a most attractive walk, the first and last parts of which are across delightful riverside meadows beside the Welland. In between you pass through two beautiful villages, and there are fine views over the valley, especially looking across to Stamford. As the town is at the far south-western tip of Lincolnshire and close to three county boundaries, there is some 'border hopping' and, although a relatively short route, it briefly enters both Northamptonshire and Rutland. Leave plenty of time to explore Stamford, one of England's most attractive and historic towns.

A 17th-century traveller described Stamford 'as fine a built town all of stone as may be seen' and this is still true today as the town is undeniably attractive and remains remarkably unspoilt. Most of its handsome stone buildings date from the 17th and 18th centuries, and it has an outstanding collection of medieval churches, whose towers and spires make a particularly fine sight when viewed from the riverside meadows on the last part of the walk. There is no single outstanding building, it is the whole harmonious package which makes a walk around Stamford so rewarding.

The walk starts in Red Lion Square. In one corner of it, at a footpath sign to The Meadows, walk along the alley called Horseshoe Lane into Sheep Market. Cross diagonally into Castle Dyke and descend to the riverside. Cross the bridge and bear half-right across

The yellow hills of Stamford

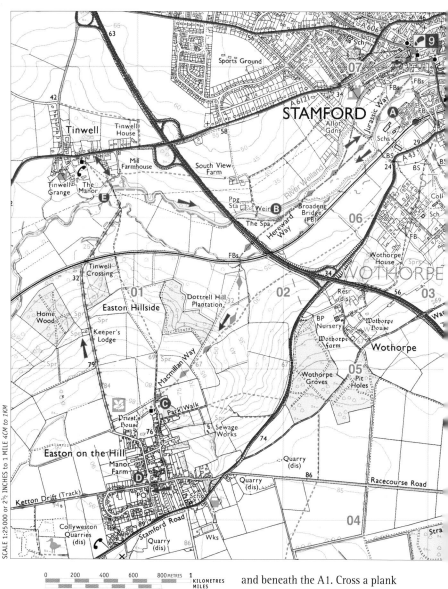

SCALE 1:25 000 or 2½ INCHES to 1 MILE 4CM to 1KM

```
0    200   400   600   800 METRES  1
                                     KILOMETRES
                                     MILES
0    200   400   600 YARDS   ½
```

the popular waterside meadow to a hand-gate in the far-right corner **Ⓐ**. Once through this, take any of the paths ahead, keeping left of the line of cables. A walk through the town meadows brings you to Broadeng footbridge. Cross this and turn right beside the River Welland.

Ⓑ In about 150 yds (137m), fork left at a post waymarked with Jurassic Way and Macmillan Way discs and walk to

and beneath the A1. Cross a plank bridge and go ahead across the field; climb to and cross a footbridge (into Northamptonshire) and *take extreme care crossing the main railway line.* Drop down the far side of the embankment; trace the path beside trees and then head up the sloping field to a gap in the belt of trees on the ridge ahead.

Beyond these bluebell woods, keep along the right-edge of the field to a corner, slip right, through a hedge-gap, and continue across the field. Climb a stile and bear right to a further stile;

once over this walk ahead across the grassy parking area to a gap in the far-left corner and turn left **C** along Church Street here in Easton on the Hill. The splendid All Saints Church is worth visiting; as with much of this picturesque village, and Stamford itself, it is built using the local Collyweston limestone that weathers so beautifully to a honeyed hue.

Walk up through the village to the main road and war memorial. Turn right and walk past the Blue Bell Inn; shortly afterwards, turn right along West Street **D**, winding with this to pass the Priest's House, a rare survival of a medieval priest's dwelling, now cared for by the National Trust. Keep right at a fork just beyond the imposing rectory; the tarred lane becomes a dirt road and drops gently from the ridge as an enclosed track, with occasional grand views across to Stamford.

At the bottom of the hill, recross the railway line and continue along an enclosed path, which bends left to a bridge over the River Welland **E**. By now the route has entered Rutland.

The walk continues to the right before crossing the bridge but for a brief detour into Tinwell, cross the bridge and immediately, at a footpath post, turn left over a waymarked stile. Head diagonally across grass – crossing a drive – climb a stile in the corner and turn right along an enclosed path. Climb a stile, follow a path across a meadow towards the church and climb another stile in the far corner. Walk along a tarmac path through the churchyard, passing to the right of the medieval church, noted for its saddle-back tower, to the main street.

Retrace your steps to the bridge over the Welland **E**, cross it and, at a public bridleway sign, turn left and keep by its meandering bank. Shortly after passing under a bridge under the A1, you rejoin the outward route **B** and retrace your steps to the start, enjoying the superb views ahead of the towers and spires of Stamford from the riverside meadows. ●

Easton on the Hill

Boston and the River Witham

Start	Boston, Market Place
Distance	6½ miles (10.5km)
Approximate time	3 hours
Parking	Boston; mostly Pay and Display
Refreshments	All services in Boston; pubs near Ⓑ and Ⓒ
Ordnance Survey maps	Explorer 261 (Boston), Landranger 131 (Boston & Spalding)

GPS waypoints

- 🥾 TF 327 441
- Ⓐ TF 332 446
- Ⓑ TF 327 472
- Ⓒ TF 303 473
- Ⓓ TF 302 472
- Ⓔ TF 323 445
- Ⓕ TF 326 440

Almost the whole of this triangular-shaped walk to the north of Boston is beside water: Maud Foster Drain, Frith Bank Drain and the River Witham. The last 2½ miles (4km) along the banks of the river are particularly attractive and memorable, especially for the impressive views of Boston Stump, the tallest church tower in the country. Leave plenty of time to explore the interesting and historic port of Boston.

Between the 12th and the 15th centuries, Boston was one of the greatest ports in England, with a flourishing trade across the North Sea and Baltic. A slump in the wool trade and the silting up of the Witham caused it to decline in the 16th century but the agricultural development of the drained Fens and subsequent dredging of the river led to its revival in the 18th and 19th centuries, and it still functions as a port. The most striking and obvious reflection of its medieval prosperity is St Botolph's Church, built in the 14th century and one of the finest and largest parish churches in the country. The spacious and lofty interior has a cathedral-like appearance but its most outstanding feature is the 15th-century tower, 272ft (83m) high and the tallest in England, always referred to as 'Boston Stump'. It is a landmark for miles around, dominating the flat landscape of the Fens and visible from many points on the Lincolnshire Wolds, around 20 miles (32km) away.

🥾 Start in the Market Place by the church and walk along Strait Bargate, which broadens out into Wide Bargate. Keep along its left side; at the traffic island take the second exit (A16 and Skegness) and cross the bridge over Maud Foster Drain. Turn left along Willoughby Road Ⓐ, passing Maud Foster Windmill, built in 1819 and the tallest working windmill in the country. Unusually it has five sails.

Continue along the road beside the drain and, just after a level-crossing, you reach a T-junction to the right of a bridge. Keep ahead through a gate, walk

0	200	400	600	800 METRES	1	
						KILOMETRES
						MILES
0	200	400	600 YARDS	½		

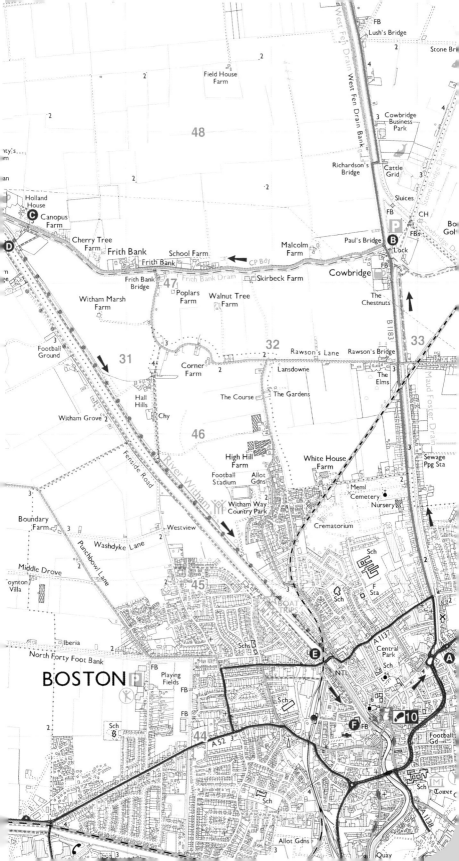

along a track and, where it ends in front of a house, turn right and follow the edge of a garden round to the left to a T-junction. Turn left – there is a junction of five drains here at Cowbridge – cross a footbridge over the Maud Foster Drain to a road and turn right. After crossing a bridge over Frith Bank Drain, turn left **B** along the road called Frith Bank, signposted for Frith Bank and Anton's Gowt. Across the fields to the left are distant views of Boston Stump.

After just over $1\frac{1}{2}$ miles (2.4km), turn left **C** at a public footpath sign to cross a footbridge over the drain, turn left along a grassy bank beside it and, at the next public footpath sign, turn sharp right along an enclosed path. Follow the path around first a left bend and then a right bend and walk through to the compacted path beside the River Witham **D**. Turn left and follow either this or the parallel grassy path on the riverbank back into Boston. Ahead there are superb views of Boston Stump almost all the time.

After passing under a railway bridge and beside Grand Sluice Lock, turn right over a bridge **E** and turn left along a tarmac path on the other bank of the river, which emerges onto a road. Keep ahead, turn left **F** to recross the River Witham via a footbridge and continue along Church Lane into the Market Place.

Boston Stump and the River Witham

Isle of Axholme

Start	Epworth, near church	**GPS waypoints**	
Distance	6½ miles (10.5km)	🥾 SE 783 039	
Approximate time	3 hours	Ⓐ SE 785 035	
Parking	Church Walk car park; free	Ⓑ SE 785 031	
Refreshments	Pubs, shops and cafés at Epworth	Ⓒ SE 780 032	
Ordnance Survey maps	Explorer 280 (Isle of Axholme), Landranger 112 (Scunthorpe)	Ⓓ SE 757 036	
		Ⓔ SE 755 048	
		Ⓕ SE 763 046	
		Ⓖ SE 769 049	
		Ⓗ SE 775 044	
		Ⓙ SE 786 044	

The Isle of Axholme is an 'island' of slightly higher ground that rises above the flat landscape of the Trent flood plain in north Lincolnshire, near the South Yorkshire and Nottinghamshire borders. This is very much 'Wesley Country' as both John Wesley and his brother Charles were born at Epworth. The walk starts by the church where their father was rector, passes the house in which the family lived and goes on to explore the pleasant countryside around Epworth, which offers wide and extensive views.

The small town of Epworth is known the world over as the birthplace of John Wesley, the founder of Methodism. His father, Samuel Wesley, was rector here from 1695 to 1735, and John was born in 1703. The attractive medieval church, in which both John and his hymn-writing brother Charles were baptised, dates mainly from the 13th century, apart from the Perpendicular tower. In later years, John was denied access because of his religious beliefs and had to deliver his powerful sermons outside, either from his father's grave or from the Market Cross. The Wesley Memorial Methodist Church in High Street was erected in 1889 in honour of John and Charles.

🥾 From the car park, take the road that leads into the Market Place and turn left along Albion Hill. At a T-junction, turn left along Rectory Street, passing to the right of the Old

Rectory. This handsome Georgian house is a later rebuilding of the one which was the Wesley family home for 40 years. It contains a large selection of Wesley memorabilia.

Just past the Old Rectory, cross to the right to find a short track Ⓐ beside a house leading to a gate into fields. Walk along the field-road, passing well-left of an old windmill. In a further 200 yds (186m), turn right Ⓑ along a raised

The Old Rectory at Epworth

path that curves gradually right to reach a road junction **C**. Carefully cross diagonally into the waymarked track beside the chapel and walk along this which continues first along the right-hand edge of fields and then heads across fields towards woodland. At a T-junction, turn left along a path, follow it around a right bend, turn left at the next T-junction and then turn right to continue along the left-hand edge of a field.

Keep ahead to pass under a disused railway bridge, continue across a field and cross a footbridge over a drain. Head across the field towards the left-end of the breeze-block barn, go through a hedge-gap here and join a path sheltered by cherry trees along the right-edge of fields. Keep a deep drain on your right, go ahead at the next path junction and continue to cross a footbridge over a junction of drains and join a rough lane. Walk along this to a junction with a tarred lane.

D Turn sharp right and walk to the far end of the woods at Epworth Turbury. Turn left along the tarred lane signed for Sandhill Farm and remain on this along the edge of the woods and around a left bend to eventually reach a corner. Turbury was the medieval right to cut peat, gorse and heather for use as fuel. Turn right along the drive, pass by the farm and keep ahead on the field road to a T-junction and waymark post.

E Turn right and trace this tractor road, Firth Lane, alongside a deep drain on your left. At the point where the track swings left across a culvert, keep ahead (with turf-fields on your right) for a further 400 yds (365m) to a flat concrete bridge **F**. Turn left across this and then bear right with the wide green path, remaining on this past

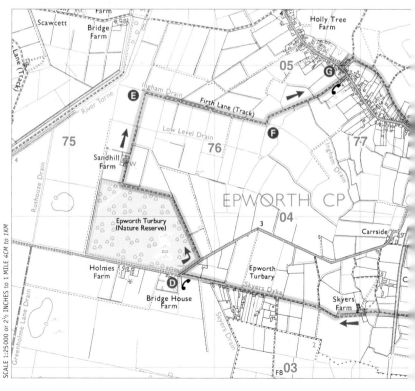

SCALE 1:25000 or 2½ INCHES to 1 MILE 4CM to 1KM

Epworth church

greenhouses to gain a village street.

G Turn left; in 100 yds (91m) turn right along a waymarked track. At the end, turn right and walk the path along the bottom edge of gently sloping fields.

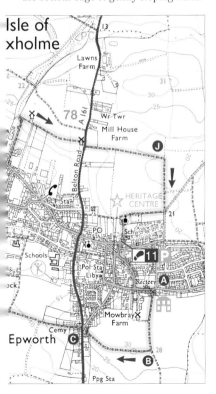

This way eventually keeps ahead beside a large new house and past a cottage, then it bends right at a waymark beside a converted chapel to reach a road. Turn left to reach the access road to an industrial area **H**. Turn left along the waymarked paved path, which shortly becomes enclosed and starts to climb. At a sharp bend, use the unusual stile on your right and walk the enclosed path to another such stile. Take this and walk to a gate into the grounds of a windmill. Do not use this but, rather, turn right and walk the field-edge path. Views south across Epworth from this modest height can be extensive.

At the main road beside a converted windmill, turn right; in 30 paces look left for the waymarked footpath along the left-edge of a field and take this wide track. Remain with this to a sharp right bend **J**, walk around this and keep ahead to reach a minor road. Turn right on a track towards the church and slip into the churchyard. The tomb of Samuel Wesley, the brothers' father, is next to the south door. Descend the churchyard access path to return to the car park entrance. ●

Frampton Marsh

		GPS waypoints
Start	Frampton Marsh; follow brown RSPB signs from Frampton	🖊 TF 363 384
Distance	6¾ miles (10.9km)	**A** TF 359 370
Approximate time	3 hours	**B** TF 346 351
Parking	Frampton Marsh; free	**C** TF 339 354
Refreshments	None en route; the Moore's Arms in Frampton is nearby	**D** TF 342 372
		E TF 349 384
Ordnance Survey maps	Explorer 249 (Spalding & Holbeach) Landranger 131 (Boston & Spalding)	

This walk visits one of the largest RSPB reserves on The Wash, a tracery of drains, salt marsh and lagoons in one of England's remotest corners. Following new and old sea-banks along the edge of the marshes, the route offers myriad opportunities to watch birds and wildfowl including (in season) some of Britain's rarest birds – marsh harriers, avocets and short-eared owls. The marshes also ripple with colourful sea lavender and sea asters in late summer, adding another dimension to this rather eerie, infinite, memorable landscape.

This south-western corner of The Wash is one of England's most important National Nature Reserves and is also listed as a RAMSAR site under an International Wetlands Conservation Convention, one of the few such sites in Britain. As with other walks in the area of The Wash, *it is best avoided on blustery winter days unless you have very effective warm and windproof clothing.* A couple of hours before high tide is the best time to do this walk (for tide information visit the website www.easytide.ukho.gov.uk).

🖊 Walk past the barrier at the rear of the car park and climb the steps up onto the embankment. Turn right through the gate and walk along the bank. Those renowned endless skies and virtually horizon-less views are a delight to behold; looking back you should see the famous 'Stump' of

Boston's church, whilst to the north a strand of wind-bent trees mark land and seashore meeting at Freiston Shore. The hazy outline of the North Norfolk coastal hills may also just be visible. Out across the salt marshes there are occasional navigation lights; closer to, old fence-lines sink into the creeks and lagoons whilst cattle complacently graze these perilous marshes.

Follow the occasionally gated embankment, which at one point turns sharply south **A** before passing above a pumping station – there's an owl box mounted on the building here. Pass by the stub end of a tarred lane and walk a further ½ mile (800m) to a fingerpost pointing right **B**; here drop off the bank, climb the stile and follow the left edge of the field past a lone apple tree – you cross the Greenwich Meridian here. At the corner turn right above the wide drain and walk through to a rough lane and path junction near Hundred Acre Farm. **C** Hop up onto the grassy embankment here, put the deep drain on your left and walk away from the farm virtually beneath the line of pylons – waymarked as Brown Fen Waterway Trail. This is a much older sea bank and a complete contrast to the one you've followed; rich with bushes, trees and a wealth of wildflowers. Cross a lane and continue along the old bank, a sinuous green path snaking through countless acres of oilseed rape and fields of grain. **D** Cross diagonally over the lane above cottages and wind with the bank over a track serving a barn complex. Upon reaching an old pillbox on your left **E** turn right on a path along Cross Bank, which arrows beside a drain straight to the current sea bank. Turn left along this to return to the steps near the car parking area. ●

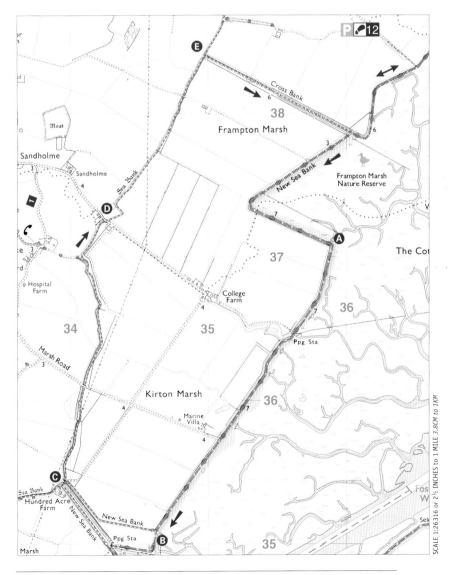

Vale of Belvoir

		GPS waypoints
Start	Woolsthorpe by Belvoir	✍ SK 837 341
Distance	6½ miles (10.5km)	Ⓐ SK 823 343
Approximate time	3 hours	Ⓑ SK 810 344
Parking	Roadside parking near village green; free	Ⓒ SK 818 359
		Ⓓ SK 843 351
Refreshments	Pubs at Woolsthorpe and Woolsthorpe Wharf	Ⓔ SK 839 350
Ordnance Survey maps	Explorer 247 (Grantham), Landranger 130 (Grantham)	

From many points on this walk on the Lincolnshire – Leicestershire border, there are fine views across the broad expanses of the Vale of Belvoir. The striking profile of Belvoir Castle is in sight for much of the way, seen from many different angles as the route describes a wide arc to the north of the castle. Almost half the walk is along the towpath of the delightful and peaceful Grantham Canal.

Woolsthorpe by Belvoir is an attractive village of ironstone cottages, presided over by a fine Victorian church.

✍ Start by the post office and small village green, turn southwards towards the church and almost immediately turn right along Belvoir Lane. Where the lane ends, keep ahead along a path and at a fork turn right and cross a brick bridge over the River Devon.

Climb a stile, keep ahead by a line of trees on the right, climb another stile and continue along the right-hand edge of a field. On this part of the walk you enjoy what are probably the finest views of Belvoir Castle, ancestral home of the earls and later dukes of Rutland. Although its towers and walls give it a medieval appearance, these were for effect only as the castle was predominantly rebuilt in the early 19th century when it was fashionable to build in a 'romantic' medieval style.

In the field corner, climb a stile and turn half right along a fieldside track,

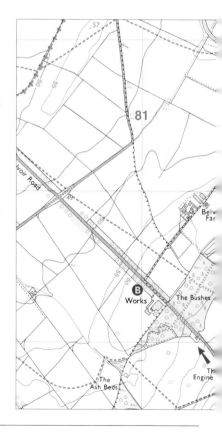

waymarked Jubilee Way, to reach a road **Ⓐ**. Turn left, follow the road around a right-hand bend and, at the castle entrance and car park, turn right along the road signposted to Redmile and Bottesford. About 220 yds (200m) past the works, turn right **Ⓑ** along a 'Dead End' lane and, after the second farm, the way continues along a rough track. Immediately after crossing a bridge over the Grantham Canal, turn right **Ⓒ** onto the towpath and keep along it for the next 2½ miles (4km).

The canal was constructed between 1793 and 1797 to link Grantham with the River Trent at Nottingham. It was abandoned in 1929, although gradual restoration is underway. This utterly peaceful section is popular with anglers and birdwatchers and passes a number of derelict locks. At the lock at Woolsthorpe Wharf – Bridge 61, The Rutland Arms – leave the canal, cross the bridge **Ⓓ** and follow the lane to a road. **Ⓔ** Turn left to return to Woolsthorpe.

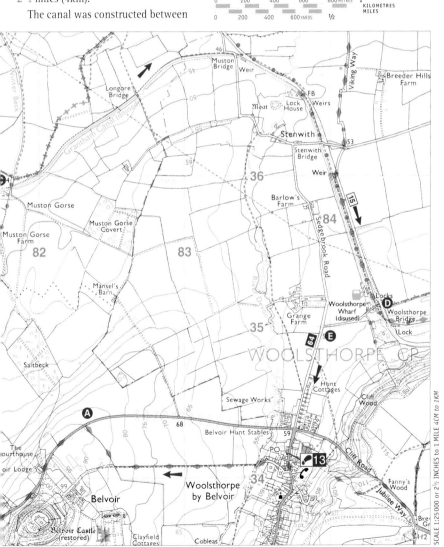

Donington and the Bain valley

		GPS waypoints
Start	Donington on Bain	TF 235 829
Distance	5½ miles (8.9km)	**Ⓐ** TF 237 828
Approximate time	3 hours	**Ⓑ** TF 248 832
Parking	Roadside, with consideration, in village centre; free	**Ⓒ** TF 234 852
		Ⓓ TF 236 860
Refreshments	Pub and shops in Donington on Bain	**Ⓔ** TF 229 858
		Ⓕ TF 228 849
Ordnance Survey maps	Explorer 282 (Lincolnshire Wolds North), Landranger 122 (Skegness & Horncastle)	**Ⓖ** TF 233 834

This fine walk begins with an easy climb onto a broad ridge and continues along the ridge, from which there are superb views over the Bain valley. It proceeds into the hamlet of Gayton le Wold and climbs again before descending into the valley, passing through the site of a deserted medieval village. The final stretch is a beautiful and r... pictu......................................

Donington on Bain is a m.............. village with a fine locatio............. Bain sheltering below the .... medieval church has a stu............... Norman tower.

The walk begins by .... and post office. Walk alor.............. passing to the right of the .... the road bears right on the .... village, turn left **Ⓐ** over a .... public footpath sign, and .... enclosed track. Head uphi.............. belt of woodland, rising to .... ridge to reach a bridleway .... a crossways **Ⓑ**. Your way ....

along the well-defined track. Off to your right at this junction, the large, shallow dishes near the transmitter are the remains of a NATO radar station at Stenigot, dismantled and abandoned here in the early 1990s. Off to your left

passing the small, brick Victorian church.

At a public footpath sign, turn left **Ⓓ** over a stile and bear left across a field to cross a footbridge. Look slightly right for a pylon in the shallow valley and walk to this to cross another footbridge.

[handwritten notes: Bolingbroke — close to E. Kirkby; P. 86]

Once over it head half-left (not ahead up the wide field road), pass between two small fenced areas and walk diagonally up across the sloping pasture, aiming just right of the giant Belmont transmitter mast. Climb a stile and turn right up an old track, rising to a stile onto a lane **E**. Turn left along the lane, in about 600 yds (550m) passing by huts and a weighbridge on your left. Just beyond these, look for a Viking Way fingerpost on the left and walk this grassy path beneath trees to use a kissing-gate into a sloping field. An information board here interprets the site of the deserted medieval village of Biscathorpe.

F Cross the footbridge at the foot of the slope and walk ahead to the lane.

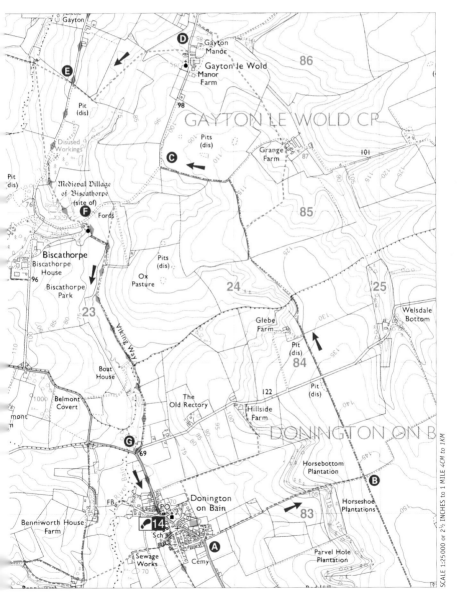

Bear left and then take the waymarked path on your right that passes immediately left of the cottage before curving right beside the ha-ha wall surrounding St Helen's Church here at Biscathorpe. This engaging little building was built in 1853 by the owner of nearby Biscathorpe House to replace a decaying medieval building. Go through the kissing-gate and turn left along a fenced track to cross a footbridge across the Bain; here turn right along a well-walked path that passes through kissing-gates and over flat bridges near to the river. At one point the Bain has been dammed to create a lake; farther along a millpond develops off to your right just before you climb a stile into a lane.

Ⓖ Turn right to the nearby junction. A few steps to the right here will reveal a good view of the old Donington Watermill (private) from the river bridge. The walk route is left at this junction to return to the nearby village centre.

The mill at Donington on Bain

Woodhall Spa

		GPS waypoints	
Start	Woodhall Spa town centre		TF 192 630
Distance	6½ miles (10.5km)	**A**	TF 186 627
Approximate time	3 hours	**B**	TF 181 637
Parking	Woodhall Spa; free	**C**	TF 108 650
Refreshments	All services in Woodhall Spa	**D**	TF 195 647
Ordnance Survey maps	Explorer 273 (Lincolnshire Wolds South), Landranger 122 (Skegness & Horncastle)	**E**	TF 200 653
		F	TF 213 648
		G	TF 196 633

A pleasant opening stretch along the Viking Way, across fields and by woodland, is followed by quiet roads and lanes. You rejoin the Viking Way for the last 1½ miles (2.4km), which is mainly through the beautiful pine and birch woodlands that surround Woodhall Spa, making an excellent finale to the walk.

Woodhall Spa developed as a small health resort in the Victorian period, when a pump room and hotels were built, but it declined after the First World War. Now it is a popular golfing and walking centre. In the Second World War it had associations with the Dambusters, and there is a memorial to them in the town centre.

Find the crossroads in the village centre (note the Dambusters Memorial in the parkland on your left), walk along

Dambusters Memorial at Woodhall Spa

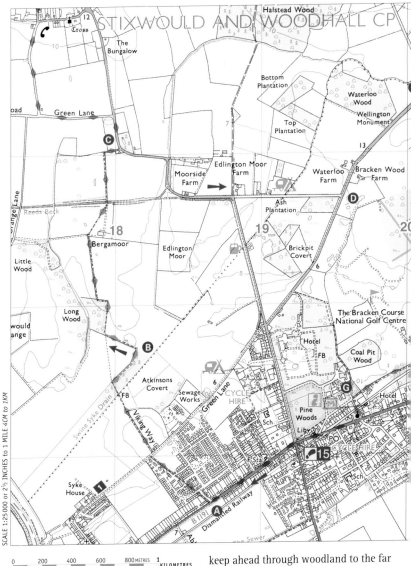

Witham Road, the B1191 signed for
Martin and Lincoln, and cross to the right.
After ¹/₂ mile (800m), and immediately
after crossing Wentworth Way, turn
right **Ⓐ** along a hedged, enclosed path
and cross straight over two estate roads
before reaching a T-junction with a
lane. Turn right and then almost
immediately left on a waymarked
(Viking Way helmet logo) track across
fields. After crossing a drain and track,
keep ahead through woodland to the far
side and turn right to a field corner.

Ⓑ Turn left in this corner and walk
to a fingerpost at the near edge of
woodland. Turn right through the hedge
gap and walk outside the woods on
your left. Turn left at the corner; at a
fingerpost turn right along a track
across fields. Cross a track near the farm
buildings, use a kissing-gate and head
half right to the low brick-built bridge.
Cross this and a nearby stile and walk
the fieldside track to a corner; here turn
right over another stile and walk to the

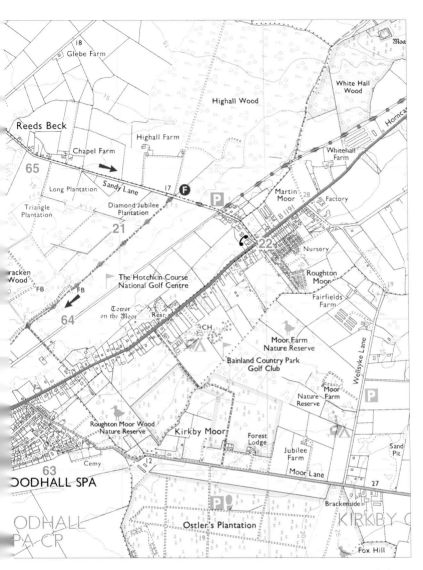

main road at the cottages.

C Turn right and follow this road around a right, then a left bend and, where it bends sharp right again, keep ahead on the lesser lane, following this through to a T-junction **D**. Turn left and walk to the next junction, noting in a field on your left a monument to the Duke of Wellington.

E Turn right at this junction and walk along Sandy Lane for one mile (1.6km). Just after reaching a major stretch of woodland, turn right at a fingerpost **F** opposite the rough lane to Highhall Cottages and go through the kissing-gate into the woods. Turn right at a T-junction along a wide path that runs beside and then across a number of golf fairways *(heed the warning signs)*, a lovely route through mixed woodlands back towards Woodhall Spa. The track eventually becomes a tarred road and passes left of a huge Edwardian mansion, continuing then as a tree-lined drive to a junction **G**. Turn left through two sets of gates, pass the tourist information centre and walk to the main road. Turn right to the village centre. ●

Bourne Wood and Edenham

Start	Bourne town centre
Distance	6½ miles (10.5km)
Approximate time	3 hours
Parking	Exeter Street or South Street, Bourne; free
Refreshments	All facilities in Bourne, pub at Edenham
Ordnance Survey maps	Explorer 248 (Bourne & Heckington), Landranger 130 (Grantham)

GPS waypoints

- 🗒 TF 095 201
- Ⓐ TF 096 205
- Ⓑ TF 091 209
- Ⓒ TF 083 210
- Ⓓ TF 067 213
- Ⓔ TF 062 217
- Ⓕ TF 078 224
- Ⓖ TF 084 203

A short and pleasant stroll from the town centre of Bourne leads to the edge of Bourne Wood. After emerging from the wood, the route continues down into the East Glen valley to the village of Edenham. The return leg takes you through the wood again. Apart from attractive woodland walking, there are grand and extensive views across the East Glen valley to the limestone hills of south-west Lincolnshire and the route is well waymarked throughout.

Bourne is one of a number of places around the Fens claimed to be the birthplace of the legendary Hereward the Wake, leader of the last Saxon revolt against the Norman conquerors. The mainly 12th-century church was once part of an abbey, founded in 1138. After the dissolution of the monasteries by Henry VIII, the nave, which had been used by the local townspeople, continued in use as the parish church.

🗒 At the town centre crossroads, face the Town Hall and turn left along North Street. Cross to the left; immediately past the Tesco garage fork left Ⓐ along the narrow Christopher's Lane. Where the tarmac ends, curve left to a fingerpost and bear right along an enclosed path to a road. Turn left to a T-junction and here turn right. As the road starts to bend left, take the signed footpath right Ⓑ, walk a few paces to

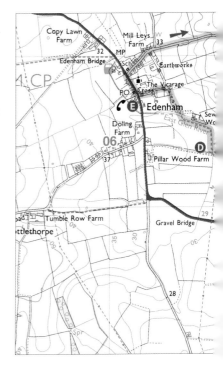

another waymark and turn left on a path between fencing on your left and a drain to your right. Go straight over the intervening road and keep ahead by the drain, then over a stile and along the right edge of a long field to reach Bourne Woods. Keep ahead to a T-junction.

ⓒ Turn right along the firm forestry track. In ¼ mile (400m), turn left at a signed path junction marked by a willow sculpture 'Helter Skelter', one of a series of living and carved artworks dotted along a sculpture trail in these woodlands. A very pleasant path strikes through broadleaf woods; keep ahead at a cross-track and continue to the edge of the woods, cross a footbridge and

turn left along the edge of a field.

Go through a hedge-gap, continue along the field edge and pass through another gap. Views from this ridge top stretch across a landscape dotted with coverts to the imposing tower of Edenham church in the valley of the River East Glen. Turn left along the top of the field and, within yards, turn right at a waymarked post and walk down its left edge. In about 250 yds (228m), skip left through a waymarked hedge gap and continue down the right edge of this field, at the foot of which cross the wide, flat tractor bridge over the East Glen.

0	200	400	600	800 METRES	1	
					KILOMETRES MILES	
0	200	400	600 YARDS	½		

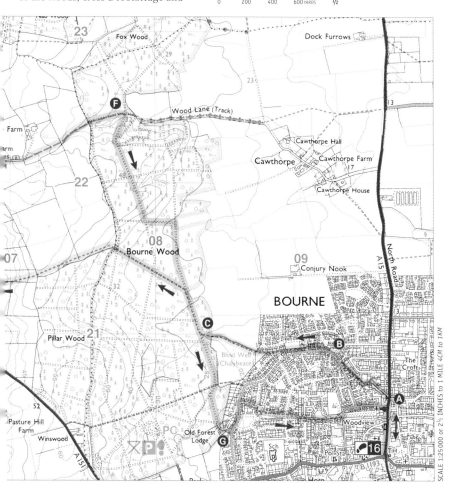

SCALE 1:25 000 or 2½ INCHES to 1 MILE 4CM to 1KM

Edenham and the East Glen Valley

D Turn right beside the water and follow it round a bend to reach and cross a narrow footbridge. Once across this, bear left along the concreted track and follow this to and over a cattle-grid, then turn left along the nearby lane to reach the main road in Edenham. **E** Turn right through the village and right again along School Lane, just past the lychgate to the village's fine 13th century Perpendicular-style church. At the fork just past the village hall and playing fields, bear right along the lesser lane. Remain on this to cross a cattle-grid just beyond a cottage. Immediately, keep ahead right onto a field road which soon reaches another cattle-grid. Here turn left, putting a hedge on your right. Climb a stile and continue towards the trees, re-entering Bourne Wood via a gate. Bear left along the main path and walk to a junction of tracks in 200 yds (182m).

F Turn right and walk this forestry road, keep ahead at a cross-track marked by a bench and then turn left at the next major junction, signed as the Lincolnshire Cycle Trail. At a T-junction turn right and stay with this forest road, keep ahead past **C** and continue to the end of the woods (signed Beech Avenue) where the track becomes tarred and bends left to reach a road.

G Turn left; walk for 250 yds (228m) and turn right along Poplar Crescent. As this bends left, walk ahead across the grass to a tarred path. Turn right, cross a bridge and turn left on a tarred path beside a brook. Remain with the path beside this brook, cross a road and swap sides of the brook, continuing through an area of new town houses. At the mini-roundabout, turn left along Exeter Street to reach the Tesco garage. Turn right to return to Bourne town centre. ●

Chapel St Leonards, Hogsthorpe and Chapel Point

		GPS waypoints	
Start	Chapel St Leonards		TF 561 722
Distance	7 miles (11.3km)	**A**	TF 554 722
Approximate time	3½ hours	**B**	TF 544 721
Parking	Chapel St Leonards; mostly Pay and Display	**C**	TF 536 721
		D	TF 535 724
Refreshments	Cafés, pubs and shops in Chapel St Leonards and Hogsthorpe	**E**	TF 531 730
		F	TF 531 738
Ordnance Survey maps	Explorer 274 (Skegness, Alford & Spilsby), Landranger 122 (Skegness & Horncastle)	**G**	TF 537 744
		H	TF 556 746
		J	TF 556 749
		K	TF 562 732

From the coast at Chapel St Leonards, the route first heads inland across fields to Hogsthorpe. It continues across reclaimed marshland, using a combination of tracks, field paths and quiet lanes, to return to the coast at Wolla Bank. A final stretch of just under two miles (3.2km) along a sandy beach, passing the slight promontory of Chapel Point, leads back to the start.

Start in the village centre at the bus station and car park. Walk inland along Sea Road, signed for Hogsthorpe and Skegness. Pass by the school entrance on your left, cross the bridge over the Orby Drain and turn immediately left along Church Lane **A**, bending right with this to reach St Leonard's Church. Enter the churchyard and keep to the right-hand edge. Just beyond the parish centre building, climb the stile on your right and turn left along the field edge. Cross a double stile and continue along the left edge of pastures to reach and

cross a footbridge and use the kissing-gate. Continue beside the drain, go through a field gate at a culverted drain and aim to walk just right of the wooden pylon in the next field, looking

A brisk North Sea breeze at St Leonards

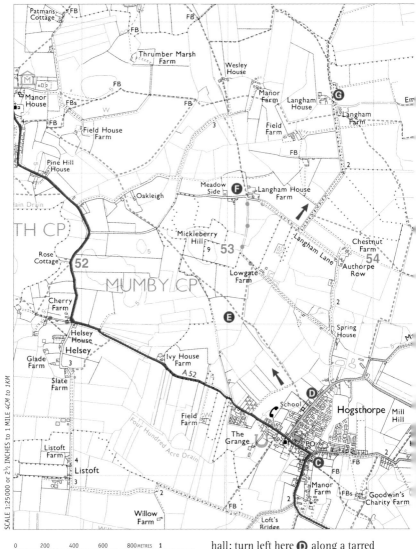

SCALE 1:25000 or 2½ INCHES to 1 MILE 4CM to 1KM

ahead for a kissing-gate amidst a stand
of trees where you join a lane.

B Turn left and wind with the quiet
lane through to a T-junction in
Hogsthorpe, near the Victoria Inn **C**.
Turn right along the main street and
walk to the village church of St Mary's.
It's well worth diverting here to visit
this fine old building. Turn along
Thames Street, beside the Saracen's
Head pub, and walk past the school.
Immediately next to this is the village

hall; turn left here **D** along a tarred
track signed as a footpath and to the
playing fields. Walk the right edge of
the enclosure and use a metal hand-
gate and steps in the first corner. Turn
half-right to a waymarked post, here
bear left alongside a drain, cross a flat
bridge and stay beside the drain. Cross a
flat tractor bridge and walk with the
drain on your right. Further plank
bridges bring you to a railed footbridge
near the corner of a tall hedge **E**. Cross
this bridge and turn right, walking
beside another drain to find a waymark
post beside a pylon. Cut the field corner

here to reach a footbridge onto a rough lane, turn left along this and follow it round to a tarred lane.

F Turn right; take the first road on the left and walk this tarred lane to a gate immediately before Langham House Farm. **G** Turn right here into Ember Lane which becomes, after a few paces, a dirt road across the old marshes. Simply remain on this; at one point it bends left to a path junction, here turn right (ignore the concessionary path ahead) and walk to a road beside the complex at Bank Farm.

H Turn left and, where the road bends left, turn right along a tarmac drive, signposted to Wolla Bank. Keep ahead through the car park and picnic area and head over the dunes to the beach **J**.

Turn right and walk along the beach to Chapel Point, where concrete steps appear **K**.

This promontory was part of the east coast defences during the Second World War, and the gun platform is still there. From here you can either continue along the beach or along a tarmac track above it to Chapel St Leonards. Where you see a road on the right, turn along it to return to the starting point.   ●

Old Bolingbroke and East Keal

Start	Old Bolingbroke		**GPS waypoints**
Distance	5¾ miles (9.3km)		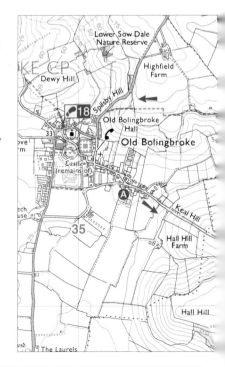 TF 348 651
Approximate time	3 hours		**A** TF 353 647
Parking	Roadside near the church; free		**B** TF 372 642
Refreshments	Pub at Old Bolingbroke, shop in East Keal		**C** TF 378 640
			D TF 382 639
			E TF 382 643
Ordnance Survey maps	Explorer 273 (Lincolnshire Wolds South), Landranger 122 (Skegness & Horncastle)		**F** TF 384 653
			G TF 371 655

The route takes you over the gentle slopes of the wolds that lie between the attractive villages of Old Bolingbroke and East Keal. There are wide and sweeping views and, as this is a walk on the south-eastern fringes of the wolds, these views extend southwards across the Fens to Boston Stump and eastwards to the North Sea coast. Historic interest is provided by the castle ruins and church at Old Bolingbroke.

Old Bolingbroke is a place of faded glories. Nowadays it is hard to envisage this small and sleepy village as a centre of royal power but in medieval times Bolingbroke Castle was a seat of the powerful House of Lancaster and the birthplace in 1366 of Henry IV, first of the Lancastrian kings. The 13th-century castle is a meagre if atmospheric ruin, comprising little more than a few low outer walls and part of the gatehouse. It declined in the Tudor period and was destroyed after the Civil War. The nearby 14th-century church is just the south aisle of a much larger structure, about three times its present size, probably built by John of Gaunt, father of Henry IV. It also suffered damage during the Civil War.

 Start by the war memorial in the village centre and walk along the narrow lane beside the Black Horse pub, which passes between the church on the left and castle ruins on the right. Follow the winding lane to a crossroads, and go straight across towards East and West Keal. Where the lane divides at miniature greens, keep on the main road, bending gently right, then left **Ⓐ** to start a steady climb up Keal Hill. Keep left at a junction and walk the long straight, enjoying fine views across this particularly pretty part of Lincolnshire, with the landmark of Boston Stump rising from the Fens far to the east.

Ⓑ At the T-junction cross to and use a hand-gate and immediately turn right through another hand-gate before angling half left across the field to a stile on the far side. Climb it and, as you continue in the same direction across the next field, you are looking across the coastal plain to the North Sea. Make for a footpath post by a hedge gap, go through the gap and head downhill across a field to a waymarked post in the trees on the far side, in-line with the tower of East Keal church. Walk through the trees, climb a stile and trace the rail fence to find a stile at the far side of this paddock. Turn right along the track; at the nearby corner fork right along the short path leading to the main road at the edge of East Keal.

Ⓒ Cross diagonally left to a hand-gate into a sloping pasture beside the driveway to 'The Manor'. Head for the diagonally opposite corner to use another hand-gate beside a cottage. Turn right down the lane; within a few paces turn left up a narrow, enclosed tarred path that climbs to a village lane. Turn right and walk to East Keal church.

Ⓓ About 75 yds (68m) before the lychgate, look on the left for a set back, enclosed, waymarked path on the left. As this issues into a field, head a touch (not sharp) left to the left-end of the spinney at the far side and a stile onto the A16.

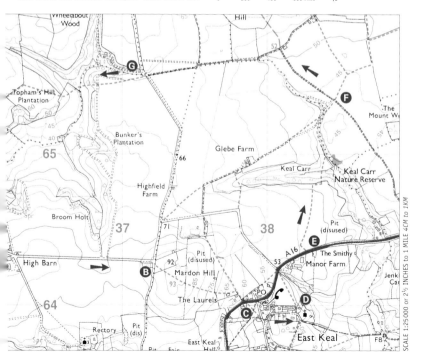

Wolds scenery near Old Bolingbroke

Turn right along the wide verge and cross to the tarred pavement. Opposite the entrance to Manor Farm shop, enter the huge field at the waymarked gateway on your left. **E** Aim to walk a hair's breadth right towards the point where the woodland dips below the near horizon. At the field edge, turn right at a fingerpost and climb the nearby stile into Keal Carr Nature Reserve. Bear half left and walk down a long series of wooden steps into the wooded valley. Follow the boardwalk, cross a brook and climb the nearby stile before walking parallel to the fencing on your right, presently reaching a gate-side stile into a farm lane. Turn right and follow this to a T-junction of tracks.

F Turn left and walk to a waymarked junction beside a barn. Here turn left on a grassy track that gradually narrows to a field-edge path, then widens again to a track between borderless fields. Keep ahead at the first fingerpost; in a further 150 yds (137m) fork left at a second fingerpost, cutting across to a hedge gap into a lane.

G Turn right; in 50 yds (46m) use a hand-gate on the left and join a field-edge track outside woodland. At a low waymark post filter left off this track on a path over the field brow to find a fingerpost, keep ahead through a wide hedge gap and head downhill to cross a footbridge on the far side of the field.

Climb a stile, head gently uphill across the next field, join a track on the far side and continue along it over the brow. At a public footpath sign, turn left and walk along the right-hand edge of the next two fields. At a hedge corner, continue across to the far side and then keep ahead along a narrow path through an area of scrub and rough grass, by a wire fence on the left. On emerging into a field, bear slightly left across it, looking out for a waymarked kissing-gate.

Go through, head quite steeply downhill and go through another kissing-gate on to a lane. Turn left and follow the lane around a left curve into Old Bolingbroke. At a junction, turn right, in the Asgarby and Hareby direction, to return to the start. ●

Lincoln and the Fossdyke

		GPS waypoints
Start	Castle Square, Lincoln	✎ SK 976 718
Distance	7½ miles (12.1km)	Ⓐ SK 969 721
Approximate time	3½ hours	Ⓑ SK 960 715
Parking	Lincoln; fees apply	Ⓒ SK 948 723
Refreshments	All services in Lincoln, Pyewype Inn at point Ⓒ	Ⓓ SK 941 738
		Ⓔ SK 948 741
Ordnance Survey maps	Explorer 272 (Lincoln), Landranger 121 (Lincoln & Newark-on-Trent)	Ⓕ SK 950 732
		Ⓖ SK 954 720
		Ⓗ SK 975 711

This figure-of-eight walk gives you the opportunity to combine many of the splendid historic and architectural treasures of Lincoln, one of England's foremost historic cities, with the pleasant countryside that lies at the foot of Lincoln Edge to the west of it. After descending from the edge, most of the route is beside the waterways of the Fossdyke and adjacent drainage channels. For much of the way the views are dominated by the towering presence of Lincoln Cathedral, and the final ¹⁄₂ mile (800m) is a steep climb to the cathedral and castle, one of the finest urban walks in the country.

Lincoln was founded as a fortress, and later a city, by the Romans at the point where the River Witham cuts through the limestone ridge of Lincoln Edge, and the city possesses one of only two surviving Roman gateways in England, the Newport Arch.

Dominating the city and much of the surrounding countryside is the majestic cathedral. The diocese was established here by the Normans in 1073, and the first cathedral was begun soon afterwards. This was almost totally destroyed by an earthquake in 1185, and the subsequent rebuilding, mainly carried out between 1192 and 1280 by a succession of energetic bishops, produced one of Europe's Gothic masterpieces. The whole of the exterior is rich in detail, and the west front is

particularly awe-inspiring, a huge 13th-century screen grafted on to some of the 12th-century arches of the original Norman cathedral. The interior is spacious and dignified and is noted for the beautiful late-13th-century Angel Choir, which was the last part of the main body of the church to be constructed, and for the intricate carvings of the choir stalls.

Next to the cathedral is the castle, founded by William the Conqueror in 1068. The curtain walls, gateways and some of the towers survive from the medieval castle but other structures date from the 18th and 19th centuries and include law courts and prison buildings. There is also a fascinating Magna Carta exhibition. Just to the south of the cathedral are the ruins of the medieval Bishop's Palace, also worth a visit.

📝 The walk begins at the top of Steep Hill and, with the castle on your left and the cathedral on your right, walk along Bailgate, passing to the right of the tourist information centre.

Turn left into Westgate to continue alongside the castle wall, at a T-junction turn right into Burton Road and almost immediately turn left along a tarred path between wide spaced walls. This bends right; then keep ahead to the right of garages, shortly reaching a road. Turn left; walk downhill to a T-junction with Yarnborough Road and turn left to the junction and traffic lights at Long Leys Road. Cross via the farthest pelican lights and look to your left for a waymarked, tarred path called Alderman's Walk.

Ⓐ Walk down this, which skirts the edge of West Common, once Lincoln's racecourse. Using gates and barriers as necessary, remain at the edge of the Common to reach the main road near tennis courts. Cross straight over and

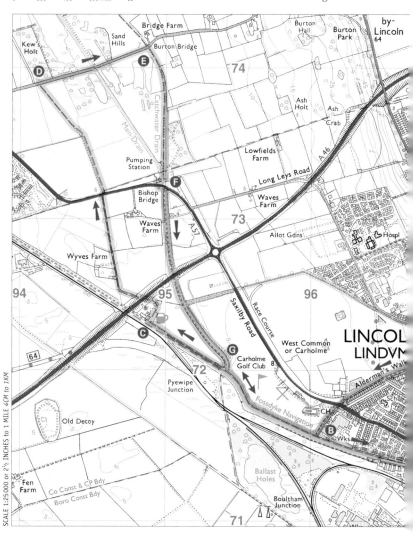

SCALE 1:25 000 or 2½ INCHES to 1 MILE 4CM to 1KM

walk the path along the left edge of Carholme Golf Course to reach a surfaced track beside Fossdyke. This canal can claim to be the oldest in the country as it was originally cut by the Romans around AD120 to link the River Witham at Lincoln with the River Trent.

B Turn right along this access road, cross a brick footbridge over Catchwater Drain and keep left beside Fossdyke to reach the Pyewype Inn. **C** Turn right through the pub's car park and bend left to pass beneath the bypass; then follow this long access lane to the main road. Cross over and walk along the right edge of a field beside a drain, cross a flat bridge in the corner and then head slightly left across the field – aim for the left edge of the bulge of woodland – to reach a lane.

D Turn right and walk along the lane, cross a bridge and continue along to the next bridge, Burton Bridge, at a corner. **E** Do not cross this, but turn right along the waymarked bridleway which traces an embankment-top route beside Catchwater Drain on your left. This is a very secluded and attractive section of the walk, with distant views through trees to Lincoln Edge and the

Steep Hill, Lincoln

Cathedral's towers. **F** At the far end turn right, cross a bridge over Main Drain and pass in front of cottages to reach a main road. Carefully cross and turn left, recross Main Drain and take the stile on the right, again putting Catchwater Drain on your left. Stay on this raised path between the drains, under the bypass and back to rejoin Fossdyke at the brick footbridge.

G Turn left and walk the waterside track to **B**; at this point stay beside Fossdyke and walk ahead towards the city, remaining beside the water on a series of paths and back streets. Upon reaching Brayford Pool, fork right to join the promenade beside the lake, which was once a busy inland port, now re-born as restaurants, bars and a university complex. At the far end, pass under the bridge and follow the River Witham towards the little 'Glory Hole' beneath High Bridge; the path jinks behind a solicitor's office before reaching steep steps up to High Street.

H Turn left, pass under the medieval Stonebow and keep ahead up the hill – first along High Street, then the Strait and finally the aptly named Steep Hill (it gets progressively steeper) to return to the start. On the way, you pass a variety of attractive old buildings, including two rare examples of 12th-century houses, and catch tantalising glimpses of the cathedral towers. ●

Walesby, Claxby and Normanby le Wold

		GPS waypoints	
Start	Walesby	🖊	TF 133 924
Distance	5¼ miles (8.4km)	**A**	TF 129 924
Approximate time	2½ hours	**B**	TF 127 931
Parking	Walesby Village Hall; free	**C**	TF 113 941
Refreshments	Seasonal tearoom in Walesby	**D**	TF 111 947
Ordnance Survey maps	Explorer 282 (Lincolnshire Wolds North), Landranger 113 (Grimsby)	**E**	TF 117 948
		F	TF 122 949
		G	TF 130 929

This is a classic wolds walk that takes you through an open and rolling landscape of broad ridges and wide valleys, with spectacular and extensive views, particularly on the final stretch between Normanby and Walesby. It is an easy route to follow as much of it is on the Viking Way. The additional ¹/₂ mile (800m) at the end to the 'Ramblers' Church' above Walesby is definitely worthwhile, both for the beautiful and atmospheric church itself and for the views over the Wolds. The gradients are all relatively easy.

Walesby is situated at the foot of the Wolds amidst some of the finest and highest scenery in Lincolnshire.

🖊 Start by turning left out of the car park to a crossroads and turn right along Moor Road. After ¹/₄ mile (400m), turn right **A** at a public byway sign, along the track to Mill House Farm and, at a fork, take the left-hand track. Climb a stile beside a cattle-grid, walk along the left-hand edge of a field, go through a gate in the corner and continue uphill along the left-hand edge of the next field to a public byway post.

B Turn left along the rutted path up the hillside. Ever-expanding views are unveiled southwards across central Lincolnshire and back along the Wolds. Pass through a gate and go ahead along the undulating field-side track, which starts to descend before curving left to reach a tarred farm lane. Turn right and walk to a minor road.

C Bear right and walk to the next corner. Look ahead here for a kissing-gate next to a field gate, go through this and trace the hedgerow through to a gate-stile. Climb this and walk beside the churchyard here at Claxby. Make time to visit St Mary's Church, which retains some nice Early English features. Continue along the lane away from the church to reach a T-junction **D**, here turn right along Mulberry Road. As it bends sharply to the right, fork left along a narrow lane, Boggle Lane, and walk to its end. Go through a kissing-gate and along a rising, grassy path, shortly skirting a vineyard before reaching another village lane, Normanby Rise.

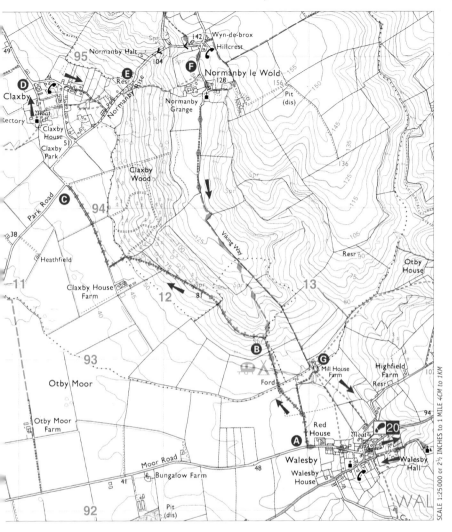

Turn left and walk uphill, passing the recreation ground on your right. Remain on the lane to the far end of Claxby Wood and look on the right for a hand-gate immediately past a small water company enclosure. **E** Go through this and continue to climb, now in a rough pasture just outside the woods. As the woods peel away to the right, look half-left for a hand-gate through the skyline hedge, go through this and walk across the pasture to the left of Normanby Grange Farm. Use the field-gate into a fenced paddock and walk to the far side where a gate allows access to a lane.

F Turn right and walk through the hamlet of Normanby le Wold; keep right at a fork to reach the little old ironstone church here in Lincolnshire's highest settlement. Remain on the track to the right of the churchyard and past the old brick hearse house, shortly climb a stile (Viking Way) and walk along the left edge of the next three fields. Extensive views take the eye south along the Wolds and to Lincoln Cathedral;

virtually straight ahead is Walesby's lonely old church on the hillside above the village.

In the third field, bend right at the corner to reach the corner of a wall. Turn sharp left here and remain beside this wall, later a hedge/fence, eventually reaching a bridlegate and fingerpost at a junction of bridlepaths. Go through the gate and keep ahead left beside the hedge, shortly reaching another bridlegate on your left. Slip through this and turn right, gradually descending a wide track beside a hedge on your right. Pass through two more gates to arrive at Mill House Farm.

Ⓖ Cross the flat bridge here and pass right of the buildings. As the driveway bends right, fork left into a meadow (used for caravans) at a rather hidden public footpath fingerpost, put a fence to your left and walk to a hand-gate in the corner. Use this and keep ahead on a well-walked path across a field, aiming just left of the large brick-built house in the distance. This path joins a hedge on your left before reaching a gated corner. Go through this and walk along the entry to reach a lane. Turn right to return to Walesby Village Hall.

It's well worth adding an additional $\frac{1}{2}$ mile (800m) to visit Walesby's redundant church of All Saints, also known as The Rambler's Church. To do so, pass by the car park and turn left on Moor Road. At the junction turn right; as this road bends sharp right, turn left along a tarred drive. Keep left at the end, joining a rougher track that rises and winds to the churchyard gates.

The church is the village's original place of worship. It marks the site of the medieval village, which was depopulated by the Black Death in the 14th century and again abandoned two centuries later. An open-access agreement means you can walk amidst the meagre lumps and furrows marking the village. The church is unspoilt inside (and was thus a favourite of both John Betjeman and Nikolaus Pevsner); the appellation 'Rambler's Church' refers to a stained glass window donated in 1951 by local rambling groups. From here retrace your path to the Village Hall. ●

The Rambler's Church, Walesby

Southrey, Bardney and Tupholme Abbey

		GPS waypoints	
Start	Southrey	🖉	TF 138 663
Distance	8½ miles (13.7km)	**A**	TF 138 668
Approximate time	4 hours	**B**	TF 116 691
Parking	Old Station car park, Ferry Road, Southrey; free	**C**	TF 119 695
		D	TF 115 703
Refreshments	Pub in Southrey, pubs and shops in Bardney	**E**	TF 123 707
		F	TF 134 688
Ordnance Survey maps	Explorer 273 (Lincolnshire Wolds South), Landranger 121 (Lincoln & Newark-on-Trent)	**G**	TF 143 683
		H	TF 150 675

There is much interest and variety on this walk on the edge of the Fens. It begins by the banks of the River Witham at Southrey and takes you across fields and by woodlands to the village of Bardney. Historic interest is provided by the churches at Southrey and Bardney and the sites of the now almost vanished medieval abbeys of Bardney and Tupholme. This is an easy and well-waymarked route with clear paths and tracks, and there is a succession of wide views.

The car park by the River Witham is on the site of the former Southrey station.

🖉 Begin by walking along the road, passing the Riverside Inn and tiny, white-painted, wooden church. The church, built in 1898, looks as if it belongs more to New England than the edge of the Lincolnshire fens.

At a Viking Way sign, turn left **A** along Highthorpe, follow the narrow lane around a right-hand bend and, at a T-junction, turn left. Where the lane peters out by a farm, keep ahead along a track that bends right. At a T-junction, turn right along the right-hand edge of a field, follow it to the left and continue along the left-hand edge of Southrey Wood. Beyond the corner of the wood, keep ahead left on the lesser track, which meanders across fields between the sugar beet refinery on the left and the outskirts of Bardney to the right. On approaching the village, turn right at a public footpath sign **B**, along an enclosed path, which bends left on to a road. Turn right along the road, passing to the left of the church, into the village centre. The 15th-century church, an attractive mixture of stone and brick, was built after the earlier church by the abbey collapsed in 1431. Some of the stones in the nave came from the abbey and some of the bricks in the chancel from Tattershall Castle.

Turn left to the road junction at the village centre. Fork right here and, immediately past the Nags Head pub, turn left **C** along Abbey Road and follow it to Abbey Farm. The mounds seen in the field ahead are all that remains of Bardney Abbey and these can be inspected more closely by keeping ahead to the parking area. The original 7th-century abbey, founded by Ethelred of Mercia, was destroyed by the Vikings in 870 and refounded by the Normans in 1087. After its dissolution by Henry VIII in the 1530s, the buildings were demolished and all that is visible on the site are some earthworks and grass-covered mounds.

D The main route turns right at a bridleway fingerpost near an old water tower and continues as a field road alongside and then across fields. At a fingerpost, keep ahead (leaving the Viking Way) to reach a road. Turn right; in about 55 yds (50m) turn left **E** along a wide grassy track, later keeping by the right-hand edge of Scotgrove Wood, to a stile. Climb it, walk along the left-hand edge of a field, parallel to a farm track, and look out for where you go through a gate to continue along the track to a road.

Cross over and take the tarmac track opposite, which curves right. After passing between a house and barn, it becomes a rough track. The track curves first left and then gradually right; pass by a fingerpost and trace the field road towards the complex of warehousing.

Southrey Wood

F At a waymark post to the left of these buildings, turn left along the left-hand edge of a field, cross a plank footbridge over a ditch and continue across the next field, making for a waymarked stile on the far side. Climb it, continue across the next field, climb another stile, in the far right-hand corner, and turn right along a narrow lane. Ahead, the ruins of Tupholme Abbey can be seen.

At a T-junction, turn right along a road and, where it bends right, turn left **G** through a kissing-gate and walk along a track, passing to the right of the abbey. This was a small monastic house, founded in the 12th century by Premonstratensian canons. There is slightly more here than at Bardney –

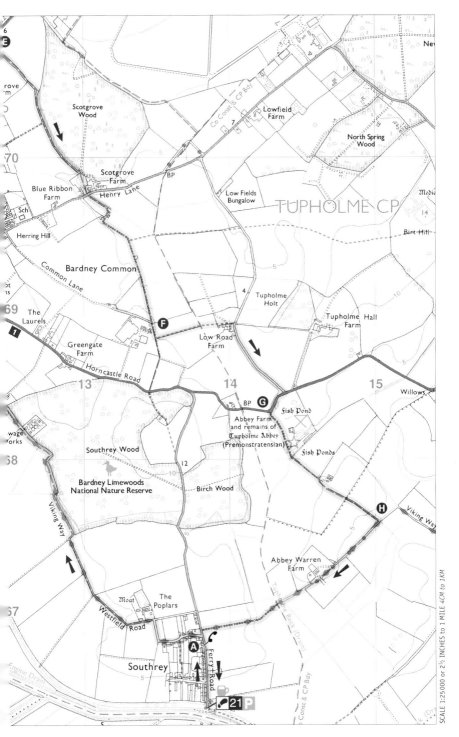

SCALE 1:25000 or 2½ INCHES to 1 MILE 4CM to 1KM

part of the south wall of the refectory.

The track later becomes hedge-lined and continues to a T-junction **H**. Turn right – here rejoining the Viking Way – and follow a track past a farm and over a footbridge to eventually emerge on to a road in Southrey. Turn left to return to the start.

Crowland and the River Welland

Start	Crowland, Trinity Bridge	
Distance	8½ miles (13.7km)	
Approximate time	4 hours	
Parking	Crowland, by the green on North Street; free	
Refreshments	Shops, cafés and pubs in Crowland, pub across Fen Bridge	
Ordnance Survey maps	Explorer 235 (Wisbech & Peterborough North), Landranger 131 (Boston & Spalding)	

GPS waypoints

- 🖉 TF 239 102
- Ⓐ TF 238 106
- Ⓑ TF 229 106
- Ⓒ TF 256 152
- Ⓓ TF 260 149
- Ⓔ TF 238 138

Almost the whole of this exhilarating walk is along embankments above either the River Welland or the parallel New River Drain. It is an entirely flat walk across a typical fenland landscape, where the views seem to stretch for ever. For most of the return leg, the tower and spire of Crowland Abbey are in sight.

The remains of Crowland (or Croyland) Abbey give some indication of the magnificence of what was one of the greatest of fenland monasteries. Particularly impressive is the ornate, partially ruined west front. Originally founded by King Ethelbald of Mercia for St Guthlac in 716, the abbey had an eventful history, being plundered, burnt and rebuilt several times. It was dissolved by Henry VIII in the 1530s, and the west front and nave of the church are the main surviving portions. The north aisle is used as the parish church.

The town grew up around the abbey and, until the draining of the Fens, the rivers ran along the main streets. This is why the streets are so wide. It also explains the presence of the unique Trinity (or Triangular) Bridge in the town centre, an impressive piece of 14th-century engineering that is now redundant. It was built at a junction of two rivers, and its three arches spanned

all the channels.

🖉 Start by Trinity Bridge at the junction of North, South, East and West Streets and walk along North Street, passing some thatched buildings and a series of greens. At a T-junction, turn left Ⓐ, follow the road around a left-hand curve and turn right along the road signposted to Deeping St James and Market Deeping. Walk along the grass verge – it is a public footpath and there are a succession of footbridges – and over to the left is 'The Lake', all that remains of a channel cut to link the town with the River Welland. It is now a picnic area.

Immediately before Fen Bridge, use two kissing-gates on your right Ⓑ, joining the embankment beside the River Welland at the village moorings. Follow this embankment-top path for

```
0      200    400    600    800 METRES  1
                                         KILOMETRES
                                         MILES
0      200    400    600 YARDS    ½
```

the next 3½ miles (5.6km). The river is rich with waterfowl and birds – look out for great crested grebe and maybe a glimpse of a day-hunting owl over the low pastures. Upon reaching a metal footbridge arcing over the river, do not cross it but, rather, turn right **C** along the rough lane and walk ahead to a

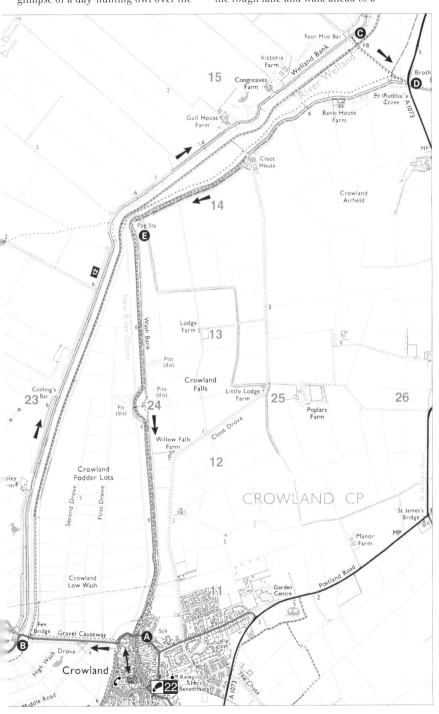

corner. Turn right over the culvert, then left over the New River Drain to continue on a track to reach a lane and main road junction.

D Turn sharp right along the narrow lane – note the roughly inscribed stump of the ancient St Guthlac's Cross on your left – and walk through to a sharp left bend near a house. Bear right off the lane here, putting wood-rail fencing on your left. Use the bridlegate and walk ahead on the wide track; then climb the embankment on your right to join a path along its top.

Shortly after climbing a stile above a pumping station, the embankment bends sharply left **E** and the tower of Crowland Abbey appears in the distance. The views across the fens are immense, a latticework of drains and field roads dappled by church spires, pylons, aerials, water towers and copses; on your right, way to the west beyond the wind-farm turbines, is a hint of an end to this fertile plain with the low hills near Stamford just discernible.

Stay on the embankment, (awkward underfoot in places where metal pilings are exposed), to reach a stile above a house. Walk ahead along the rough lane and carefully cross the road into North Street to return to the Trinity Bridge in Crowland. ●

The west front of Crowland Abbey

Barnetby le Wold, Bigby and Somerby

		GPS waypoints
Start	Barnetby le Wold	
Distance	6¾ miles (10.9km)	🖉 TA 056 098
Approximate time	3 hours	Ⓐ TA 056 096
		Ⓑ TA 056 091
Parking	Roadside near Barnetby le Wold Post Office or stores; free	Ⓒ TA 059 073
		Ⓓ TA 067 065
Refreshments	Pub and shops at start	Ⓔ TA 085 078
Ordnance Survey maps	Explorer 281 (Ancholme Valley), Landranger 112 (Scunthorpe & Gainsborough)	Ⓕ TA 074 095
		Ⓖ TA 064 094

The route follows the Viking Way southwards from Barnetby le Wold, passing through the hamlets of Bigby and Somerby, before heading up onto the gentle, fresh and open slopes of the northern wolds. The extensive views from here include the Ancholme valley to the west and extend to the industries of Humberside on the eastern horizon.

Barnetby le Wold is mainly a creation of the Victorian railway era, situated at the junction of three lines, but the semi-derelict Norman church on the south side of the village is evidence of an older agricultural settlement.

🖉 Start in the main street by the post office and, facing it, turn right and take the first road on the right (St Mary's Avenue). Just before the road ends, turn right onto a tarmac track, which soon becomes a rough, fence-lined track. The first part of the walk follows the well-waymarked Viking Way. At a junction of tracks Ⓐ keep ahead right along the bridleway, putting a rail-fence on your left. At the fork continue straight along the wider way to reach a narrow lane. Turn left and, where the lane curves left, turn right Ⓑ at a public footpath sign, along an enclosed track.

The track heads in a straight line across fields and, where it ends, bear slightly left on to a faint path across a field to a footbridge on the far side. Cross it, keep ahead across the next field to a T-junction, turn right and, at a waymarked post, turn left to continue along the right-hand edge of a field. Bear left on meeting a track, turn left at a T-junction and, at a public footpath sign, turn right along the right-hand edge of a field. In the corner, cross a footbridge over a ditch, turn right to cross another one and turn left along the left-hand edge of the next field.

Follow the track around a left-hand bend to a T-junction, turn right along a tarmac lane and follow the lane around a left-hand bend to another T-junction, in the hamlet of Bigby Ⓒ. The 13th-century church is to the left. Turn right along the road to reach a T-junction. Cross straight over and use the kissing-gate; then trace the well-worn path to two more gates and a footbridge.

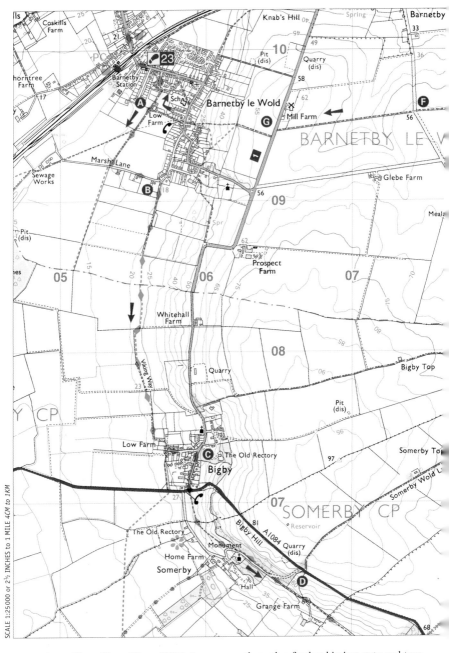

SCALE 1:25000 or 2½ INCHES to 1 MILE 4CM to 1KM

0   200   400   600   800 METRES   1
                                    KILOMETRES
                                    MILES
0   200   400   600 YARDS   ½

Continue uphill to pass beside the slender monument erected in 1770 to celebrate the 29th wedding anniversary of Sir Edward and Ann Weston of nearby Somerby Hall.

At the far side of the sloping field go through a further kissing-gate and turn left up the narrow, wooded lane, passing to the left of Somerby's small medieval church. The west tower is scarcely higher than the roof. At a fork, continue along the left-hand lane – here leaving the Viking Way – which curves left gently uphill through trees to a crossroads **D**. Take the lane ahead,

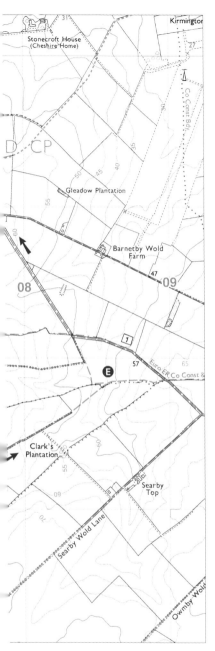

Wolds near Barnetby

corner and some bridleway fingerposts. **E** Turn sharp left; then in 50 paces turn right at another bridleway fingerpost, walking alongside the new hedge on your right. Keep ahead at the next junction, rising gently to a further junction where again you go ahead, joining a very wide green swathe signed as National Cycle Route 1. At a house this becomes a tarred lane; go forward to a junction and here keep ahead right on the road to a right-hand bend. **F** Turn left at the fingerpost here, skirting the left-hand edge of the huge field. In the far corner use a stile to enter a paddock and then another into a road.

G Turn left; within a few paces turn right along the left edge of a sloping field, dropping towards Barnetby. Climb another stile and aim slightly left *(not half-left)*, dropping down just left of the line of pylons to find a stile in the bottom left corner just below a pond. Climb this stile and walk along the track to the left of white-painted cottages to reach a lane. Cross straight over and walk the roughening track past more houses, shortly reaching **A**. Here turn right to walk the initial short stage back to the start.

signposted to Somerby Top, which heads over Somerby Wold. Beyond Somerby Top Farm, it continues as a rough track and, where it bends right, keep ahead, at a public bridleway sign, along the right-hand edge of a field.

Remain on this well-used bridleway, dropping down into a shallow combe to reach the near end of a newly hedged

Around Horncastle

			GPS waypoints
Start	Horncastle		🖉 TF 258 696
Distance	9 miles (14.5km)		Ⓐ TF 267 699
Approximate time	4 hours		Ⓑ TF 273 710
Parking	Horncastle; free		Ⓒ TF 272 718
Refreshments	All services in Horncastle, pub by Shearman's Wath Bridge		Ⓓ TF 240 713
			Ⓔ TF 234 708
Ordnance Survey maps	Explorer 273 (Lincolnshire Wolds South), Landranger 122 (Skegness & Horncastle)		Ⓕ TF 236 699
			Ⓖ TF 236 688
			Ⓗ TF 242 677
			Ⓙ TF 257 680
			Ⓚ TF 254 693

The walk is a lengthy and wide circuit of the Bain valley to the north, west and south of Horncastle, and the first and last parts are along the Viking Way. It is a mainly flat walk at the base of the Wolds, and the views westwards extend to the long ridge of Lincoln Edge, with the towers of Lincoln Cathedral visible on the horizon. The final stretch is a relaxing stroll beside the Horncastle Canal. Expect mud in some places after wet weather.

Horncastle is situated on the site of a Roman fort, and there are a few remaining fragments of the Roman walls, one of which is incorporated into the structure of the library. Nowadays the town is renowned as an antiques centre. The church, built from the local greenstone, dates mainly from the 12th and 13th centuries, though it was heavily restored in Victorian times.

🖉 Find the Market Place and, with your back to the Post Office, turn left along the main High Street. At the crossroads go straight over into narrow Banks Street, shortly walking alongside the little River Waring. Where a concrete footbridge crosses the river, ignore this and, rather, turn left up Linden Road. Turn first right (The Becks) and go diagonally over at the crossroads, joining Bowl Alley Lane. At the point where this bends left, fork ahead along a wide, enclosed path. At the far end of the housing, turn left Ⓐ at a fingerpost and trace the path to a kissing-gate into a lane.

Turn right along the lane and keep left at the junction. In a further ½ mile (800m), take the waymarked bridleway (Viking Way) to the left, opposite a lane to Low Toynton Ⓑ. Cross a drain and continue to the next field corner; turn right along the left field edge and walk to the far end of the hedge. Turn left here along a fieldside track; in 150 yds (137m) bend right with this track alongside a drain. The path swaps sides of this drain before reaching a T-junction of field roads. Ⓒ Turn left (leaving the Viking Way) and follow this undulating track through to the main road at the edge of West Ashby.

Cross carefully and continue along the lane opposite for 1½ miles (2.4km), passing the Golfers Arms public house

The Horncastle Canal

and crossing the River Bain to reach the busy A158 **D**. Again cross carefully and take the track opposite across fields, later keeping along the left-hand edge of woodland. At a public bridle-way sign, where the edge of the wood bears right, keep straight ahead across the field to a footpath post on the far side **E** and turn left along a path, passing along the left-hand edge of a solitary clump of trees. Keep straight ahead across the field towards the houses of Thimbleby, making for a footbridge over a ditch, cross it and continue to a stile on the far side. This accesses a narrow, tarred path between bungalows that leads to the village road in Thimbleby **F**. Cross straight over into Chapel Lane and walk ahead past the derelict Wesleyan Chapel. Go straight ahead across a track, joining a waymarked field path that drops gently to cross a plank bridge just left of a spinney. Continue uphill in the same direction, rising easily to a stile into a lane. Turn right into tiny Langton, walking past the little church and Manor House.

G Immediately past the entrance to Langton Manor farmyard, turn left along a narrow, enclosed, waymarked path. Climb the stile and keep ahead, shortly walking by a fence beside a farm track on your left. Climb two stiles in close succession and join this track, walking ahead along the left, then right edge of fields. In 500 yds (457m) the track bends left; here, keep straight ahead on a lesser track. This passes just left of a farm reservoir and then rises up the slope, heading directly for the distant, multi-gabled house in the trees on the skyline. At the top of the slope you'll rejoin the wider field road; turn right and walk to a lane beside a cottage, here turn left to reach the main road.

H Turn left through the hamlet of Thornton. Where the main road bends sharply left, carefully cross to the right to join a tarred lane that meanders through typically huge arable fields, with Horncastle and the distant Wolds as a backcloth. Pass an old railway building and, immediately, cross a bridge over the abandoned Horncastle Canal. **J** Turn left through a kissing-gate to join a waterside path alongside the old waterway (closed in 1885), walking past a derelict lock on your left.

Remain beside the waterway, walking through meadows to reach a kissing-gate in a corner; use this and walk ahead to the near end of a footbridge. **K** Do not cross this bridge, but bear right along the tarred access road to the sports centre, a tree-lined route that brings you to a bridge across the canal at a main road. Carefully cross at the pelican crossing here and walk along the pretty lane opposite to reach the churchyard and St Mary's Square. Bear right to return to the nearby Market Place. ●

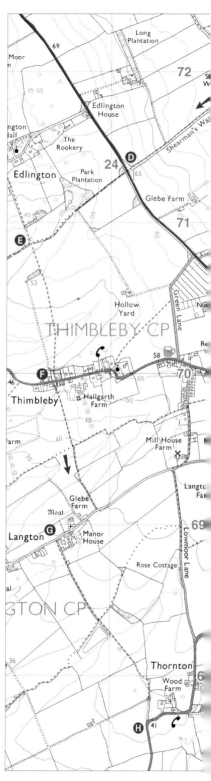

| 0 | 200 | 400 | 600 | 800 METRES | 1 |
| 0 | 200 | 400 | 600 YARDS | ½ | KILOMETRES MILES |

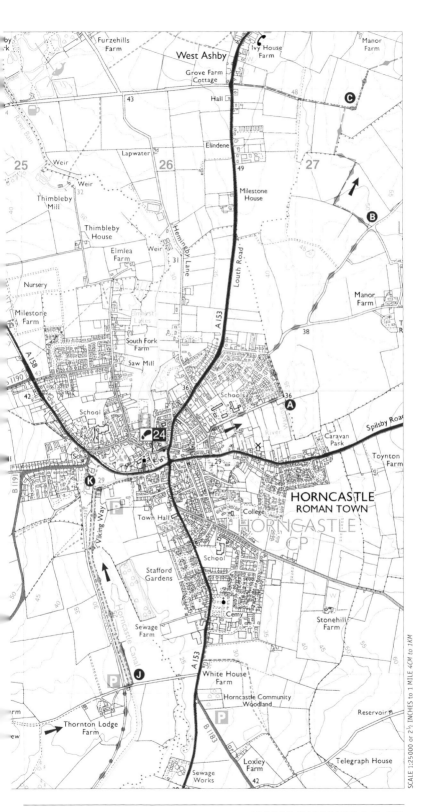

Top of the Wolds

		GPS waypoints
Start	Caistor	✏ TA 118 014
Distance	8 miles (12.9km)	Ⓐ TA 117 009
Approximate time	3½ hours	Ⓑ TF 113 996
Parking	Town Hall car park; free	Ⓒ TF 122 984
Refreshments	Pubs and shops in Caistor, pub and shop in Nettleton	Ⓓ TF 114 969
		Ⓔ TF 110 992
Ordnance Survey maps	Explorer 282 (Lincolnshire Wolds North), Landranger 113 (Grimsby)	Ⓕ TF 108 997
		Ⓖ TA 109 002
		Ⓗ TA 101 009

Caistor stands in a fold in the western scarp of the chalk ridge and is flanked by typical rounded shoulders and tops of the Wolds, incised by steep-sided, winding valleys and bournes. This walk leaves the old Roman town to explore one of these great gashes in the hills before rising to one of the best viewpoints in Lincolnshire at Nettleton Top; an immense panoramic sweep across the heart of England and north towards the distant Yorkshire Wolds.

✏ Take the ramped path down beside the Town Hall, cross High Street and walk to the Market Place. Head straight across the square, joining a road signed for the A46 and as the Viking Way. Keep left on Horse Market, bend right along Nettleton Road and cross to the left as a road joins from the left. In 100 yds (91m), turn left along the enclosed, waymarked path behind bungalows, go ahead at the end and turn left into a cul-de-sac. Look for the narrow, fenced path on the left that winds around the rear of housing to rise to the bypass.

Ⓐ Carefully cross, descend the ramp opposite and enter a field. Trace the left edge into the next field; then look ahead for a kissing-gate just in from the corner. Use this and walk the right edge of several fields. At a final kissing-gate head half left to pass left of a bungalow's gardens, reaching a lane at

a corner. Bear right to a T-junction in Nettleton. Turn left to follow Normanby Road for about 600 yds (550m) to a fork Ⓑ, here take the lane to the left, signed as a bridleway and the Viking Way. Keep left before the stables, cross the brook and turn right at a fingerpost on to a field path. Pass left of the pool and keep right at a waymarked post, cross a flat bridge and follow the path alongside Nettleton Beck.

Several stiles and gates take the path along the secluded valley, rising gently to a hand-gate onto a steep concrete track Ⓒ. Turn uphill, pausing to enjoy this peaceful land of fox coverts, marsh, dry valleys and hill top woods. In about 150 yds (137m) take the waymarked path on the right, dropping down a wooded path to reach some bricked-off

0	200	400	600	800 METRES	1	
						KILOMETRES
						MILES
0	200	400	600 YARDS	½		

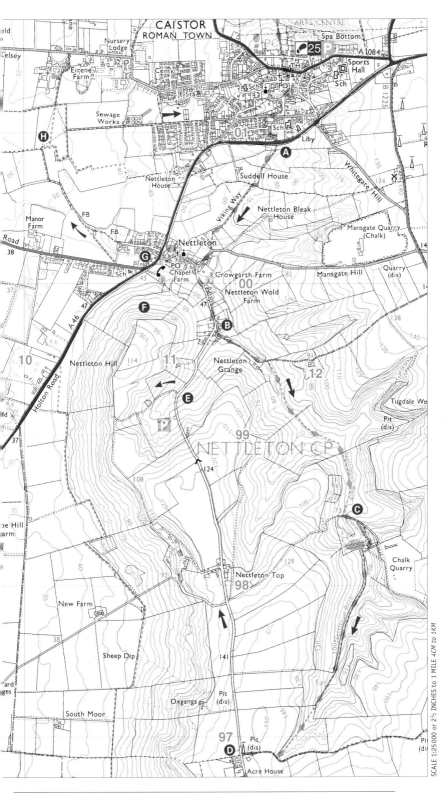

tunnels on the left. These are reminders of the ironstone mining industry that riddled these hills until 1968; the tunnels were adits into the hillside where narrow gauge railways brought out the hard-won rock from underground levels.

Use two hand-gates and rejoin the beck-side path. The valley gradually shallows as the route rises; most of the grassy terraces, banks and mounds are spoil from the old mines, now long-returned to nature and rich with wildflowers in spring and summer. At the beck spring, use the hand-gate and head slightly right, continuing up the declining valley, eventually reaching a corner, gate and stile marked by bridleway and Viking Way signs. Turn right through this and walk the track through to a road. Look back left here; between you and the radar dome is Lincolnshire's highest point at 168m (551ft).

D Turn right along the quiet, ridge-top lane, which runs virtually level for well over a mile. On clear days the views are magnificent, west across the Vale of Trent to the distant smudge of the Peak District and (after a while) back left to Lincoln Cathedral. To the east the Wolds ripple away towards the coast. The lane

Nettleton Beck Valley

descends and passes a rambler's car park. At the bend 150 yds (137m) later **E**, take the gated track on the left (the second gate here) – there's a nettle-leaf waymark disc – and walk past the huge corrugated-iron barn, continuing uphill to reach a corner. Take the stile on the right and join a ridge-top path.

The path is marked by a line of waymarked posts; presently the route turns sharp right at a corner and reaches a waymark post **F**. Here, turn left and drop steeply downhill. Several more posts point right beneath cables, then left, bringing you to a stile just above the large house; use this and walk beside the hedge (right) to reach the main road. Turn right into Nettleton.

G Turn left opposite The Salutation pub along Cooks Lane. Go ahead through bollards at the end and walk just left of a new house, towards the brick pumping station ahead. Cross a footbridge, pass right of the compound and take another bridge, walking alongside the brook to a kissing-gate. Walk the wide, green track to another kissing-gate beside a pine tree, use this and walk the right edge of a field, cross a drain and turn right to a nearby fingerpost.

H Remain beside the ditch, following the path around a right, then two left bends to reach another fingerpost. Turn right and walk this long track, then road (Navigation Lane), back into Caistor. At the far end turn left down Cromwell View, keep right and then wind up to the church. Keep this on your right, pass Caistor School and bend left to the High Street. Up to your right is The Talbot, behind which is the Town Hall car park. ●

Tealby and Kirmond le Mire

		GPS waypoints
Start	Tealby Village Hall	TF 158 908
Distance	7¼ miles (11.7km)	**A** TF 168 902
Approximate time	3½ hours	**B** TF 180 895
Parking	Car park behind village hall; free	**C** TF 177 906
Refreshments	Shop, tearoom and pubs in Tealby	**D** TF 187 925
Ordnance Survey maps	Explorer 282 (Lincolnshire Wolds North), Landranger 113 (Grimsby)	**E** TF 171 930
		F TF 172 934
		G TF 160 914

From the attractive village of Tealby, this well-waymarked route takes you across a quiet, open and rolling landscape that is typical of the Lincolnshire Wolds. Most of the way is on clear paths and tracks, and there are fine and extensive views.

The picturesque village of Tealby, situated on the lower slopes of the Wolds above the little River Rase, has a thatched pub, attractive old cottages and an ironstone church that mainly dates from the 14th and 15th centuries. It was the home of the Tennyson d'Eyncourt family, who were related to Lord Tennyson, but their grand 18th-century house, Bayons Manor, was demolished in the 1960s.

From the car park entrance turn left down Beck Hill, dropping to use a footbridge beside a ford. Keep ahead along the tarred lane beyond, pass a farm, go straight over a cross-track and wind easily uphill, past a bungalow and, shortly, a derelict lodge house to Bayons Manor. The roughening lane drops into a dip; turn right here **A** on a waymarked path along the right edge of a field.

At a field corner bend left, pass through a hedge gap at the next corner and in a further 50 paces, turn right as waymarked up a steep bank, then trace the right edge of a field around to a fingerpost. Turn right and walk the left edge of this field; look out for Lincoln Cathedral as a focal point on the

Tealby

horizon. At a T-junction, turn left along a field road to reach the main road opposite High Street Farm. **B** Turn left and, after almost ¾ mile (1.2km), turn right through the gates of Kirmond Hall Estate **C** and walk along a straight, tarmac track. Where the track bends right, keep ahead, at a public bridleway sign, to join another track, which keeps along the right-hand edge of a field. Look out for where a blue waymark directs you to bear left through a gate and follow a path gently downhill through a shallow, U-shaped valley, later keeping by a wire fence on the left.

Go through a handgate in the fence and continue by the fence on your right, shortly allowing this to drift away as you take the bridlepath straight across the field towards the distant buildings. **D** These are at Kirmond le Mire Manor Farm; turn left up the road and carefully cross to the right to take the bridleway running beside the little Victorian church here. At the nearby T-junction turn left onto a fieldside track which shortly bends right before dropping through a neck of woodland and down into a shallow valley. Upon reaching a lane, turn right **E** and after ¼ mile (400m) turn sharp left **F** along a waymarked field path beneath pylons.

Cross the main road and join the waymarked path opposite, walking to the right of a hedge and then above a hollow. Cross a flat bridge, use a kissing-gate and rise to another such immediately right of the copse. A wide field track slices ahead across the field; at the point this bends left, fork right to a nearby gap-stile into a lane. **G** Bear left and walk this down into Tealby. Keep left of the churchyard and go straight over the crossroads to return to the village hall. ●

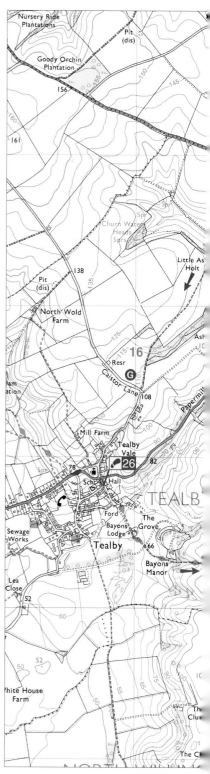

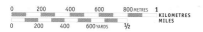

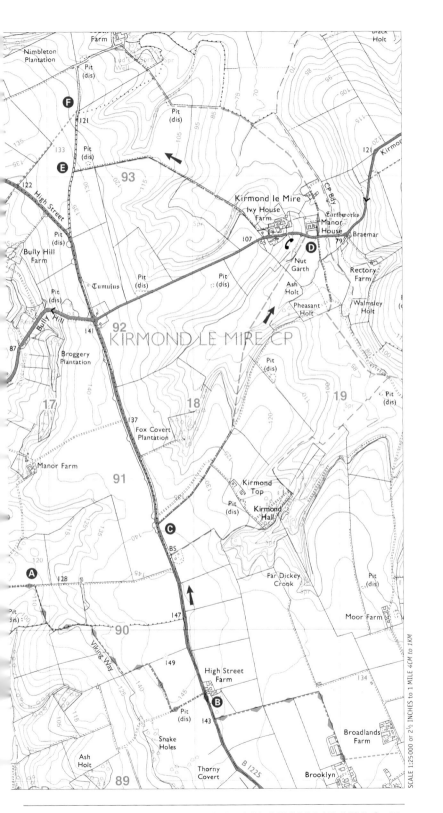

SCALE 1:25000 or 2½ INCHES to 1 MILE 4CM to 1KM

Laceby, Irby upon Humber and Aylesby

Start	Laceby
Distance	7¾ miles (12.5km)
Approximate time	3½ hours
Parking	Laceby Village Hall car park; free
Refreshments	Pubs and shops in Laceby
Ordnance Survey maps	Explorer 284 (Grimsby, Cleethorpes & Immingham), Landranger 113 (Grimsby, Louth & Market Rasen)

GPS waypoints	
🖋	TA 213 065
Ⓐ	TA 211 061
Ⓑ	TF 217 047
Ⓒ	TF 209 042
Ⓓ	TF 213 036
Ⓔ	TF 202 030
Ⓕ	TF 201 043
Ⓖ	TA 195 050
Ⓗ	TA 202 075

This highly attractive and enjoyable walk takes you across gently rolling country on the eastern slopes of the Wolds and passes though three pleasant villages, all of which have medieval churches. There are superb views both over the Wolds and across the flat country to the north and east that borders the coast and Humber Estuary.

Laceby is situated on the edge of the Wolds just inland from the built-up area of Grimsby and Cleethorpes. The church dates mainly from the 12th and 13th centuries and has a fine 13th-century tower.

🖋 From the car park, turn right along High Street and, at a T-junction, turn right again along Caistor Road. The road bends right and later curves left to the busy A46. Cross carefully, turn left and, at a public bridleway sign, turn right Ⓐ along a tarmac track (Lopham Lane). Beyond the last of the houses the lane becomes a rough fieldside road; keep straight on as it becomes a grassy track that eventually emerges on to a lane. Cross the lane and the footbridge and turn right along the parallel tarred lane to reach a road.

Ⓑ Cross straight over to join the waymarked Wanderlust Way, tracing the line of a drain along the right edge of fields. Cross a footbridge and continue ahead to the distant corner; here turn left to the next corner and then right to rise gently to a tarred lane near houses. Ⓒ Turn left and walk past Hilltop House, remaining with the track as it roughens and follow it for around ½ mile (800m) to a T-junction.

Ⓓ Turn right at the Wanderlust Way fingerpost and put the hedge to your immediate left. At a fork keep ahead right along the waymarked bridleway, aiming to arrive at the left corner of the distant woodlands. Keep ahead; the path runs within the edge of Irby Holmes Wood, which is thick with woodland wildflowers in spring. Stay with the path as it descends beyond the woods and then rises to a fingerpost.

Ⓔ Turn right, putting a hedge on

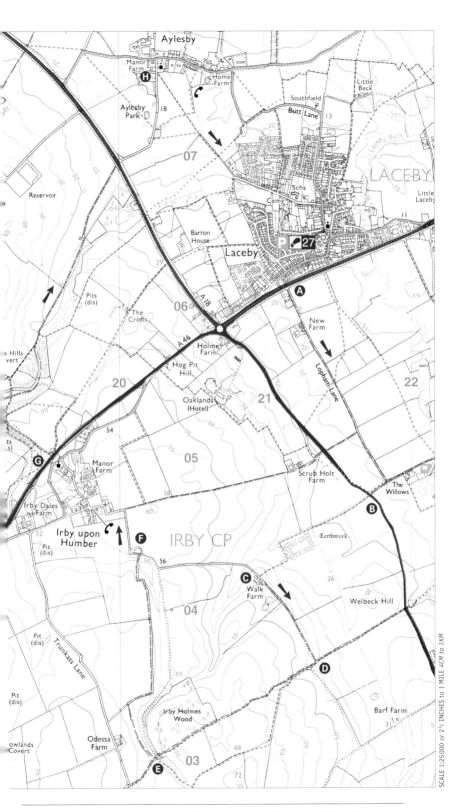

SCALE 1:25 000 or 2½ INCHES to 1 MILE 4CM to 1KM

The church at Irby upon Humber

your left. At the next corner again turn right along the field edge, back towards the woods, shortly reaching another corner. Here turn left and keep beside a hedge along the right edge of fields. Off to your right are the distant chimneys of industrial Immingham and also the tall, graceful brick tower at Grimsby Docks. This fieldside track eventually reaches a corner, where a gap in the hedge at the top of a bank gives access to a tarred lane.

F Turn left, follow the lane around a series of bends into Irby upon Humber – despite its name it is over four miles (6.4km) from the river – and at a road junction, turn right along Church Lane to the church. Apart from the tower, much of this medieval church was rebuilt during an extensive restoration in 1863. Turn left at the T-junction; turn right along a track down to the A46. Cross carefully, turn right and then turn left along the entry immediately before Rowells Cottage **G**. Go through a kissing-gate and join an enclosed track that skirts the upper edge of a deep valley, the start of a delightful section of route with pleasant views of the Wolds.

The path curves right and descends to a cross-track in the valley bottom. Keep straight ahead, now rising and bending gradually right to reach a kissing-gate into Rush Hills Covert. Walk along the inside edge of the woods, shortly dropping to a junction where you bear left; then turn right to walk immediately outside the trees to reach and use a bridlegate into pasture. Keep to the left edge, above a stream, and as this dries at a culvert, continue alongside the trees and then along a field road to stock-pens at the end of the field. Two gates here lead into an enclosed track; follow this to the main A18 dual carriageway.

Carefully cross straight over into the 'No-Entry' lane (Temple Lane) and follow this through to Aylesby village. The church here has a Perpendicular tower with some fine gargoyles; it was, like those at Laceby and Irby, much restored in Victorian times. Just before the church is a fingerpost on the right **H**, pointing the way back to Laceby along a tarred footpath. Remain on this to a barrier, beyond which an enclosed path emerges into a lane. Keep ahead on this before bending left to pass by housing and the village school. At the T-junction turn right to return to the centre of Laceby.

Four Lincoln Edge villages

		GPS waypoints
Start	Wellingore	🖊 SK 981 568
Distance	8½ miles (13.7km). Shorter version 6½ miles (10.5km)	Ⓐ SK 985 578
Approximate time	4 hours (3 hours for shorter walk)	Ⓑ SK 969 577
		Ⓒ SK 971 588
Parking	Wellingore Memorial Hall; free	Ⓓ SK 956 587
Refreshments	Pubs and shops in Coleby, Navenby and Wellingore	Ⓔ SK 959 593
		Ⓕ SK 966 601
Ordnance Survey maps	Explorer 272 (Lincoln), Landranger 121 (Lincoln & Newark-on-Trent)	Ⓖ SK 975 603
		Ⓗ SK 986 589

The four attractive villages – Wellingore, Navenby, Boothby Graffoe and Coleby – lie along a 3-mile (4.8km) stretch of the limestone ridge of Lincoln Edge or Cliff. The route descends from the ridge at Navenby, continues across fields at its foot, climbs back up to it at Coleby and then follows the Viking Way along the ridge back to the start. From both the top and the foot of the ridge, there are fine and extensive views. The shorter walk omits the opening and closing section between Wellingore and Navenby.

🖊 Starting in the Memorial Hall car park, walk to the left of the hall (past the noticeboard), past a derelict stile with a Viking Way disc and through the area of slides and swings to a kissing-gate in the corner. Beyond this follow the obvious path across scrubland to another kissing-gate; turn right beyond this and walk the fenced path along the top of the sloping pastures.

Use a hand-gate and remain on this path to take a kissing-gate into the edge of woodland. Turn right to trace the well-worn path beyond the woods, then along the right-hand field edge, around two sharp bends and through a gate into a tarred lane in Navenby. At a public footpath sign, turn left along a tarmac track called The Smoots and, where it ends, keep ahead along an enclosed, tree-lined path. Follow it around a left-hand bend and, at a

public footpath sign, turn right through a kissing-gate.

Continue along an enclosed path, go through another kissing-gate, turn right and almost immediately left over a stile. Walk across a field towards Navenby church and climb a stile onto a lane Ⓐ.

If starting the walk at Navenby, walk down Church Lane from the main road to pick up the full walk here.

Turn left downhill, follow the lane around right- and left-hand bends, cross a bridge over a disused railway line and, after a further ½ mile (800m), turn right Ⓑ along a straight, hedge-lined track. Later keep along the left-hand edge of fields, follow the track around right- and left-hand bends and continue to a narrow lane Ⓒ. Turn left and, after nearly one mile (1.6km), turn right at a public footpath sign in front of a house Ⓓ. As you walk along the left-hand edge of a field, glimpses of Somerton Castle can be seen over to the left. The castle was built in 1281 by a bishop of Durham but only a tower survives from this medieval building, incorporated into the present 17th-century farmhouse.

Turn right in the waymarked field corner and continue along its left-hand edge beside a drain and hedge. Cross a culvert, putting the hedge and drain on your right, and keep ahead, shortly bending left to a fingerpost and field road. Walk along this towards the pylons to reach a T-junction. Here turn right **E**, cross a plank bridge and remain with the drain on your right. At the second low waymarked post turn left, putting a lesser drain on your right, and meander with this field road beside and across fields; it becomes an enclosed track before reaching a road.

F Turn right and follow the road, re-crossing the old railway before starting to climb up onto Lincoln Edge, shortly reaching the village green in Coleby. *A short diversion left, past The Tempest Inn, leads to the village's fine medieval church;* otherwise, the main route turns right at a fingerpost **G** along a narrow, enclosed path, here rejoining the Viking Way for the rest of the route.

The path bends to a junction; here keep ahead right along the narrow way,

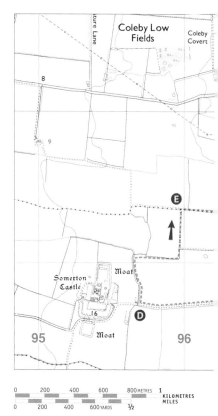

presently emerging onto a path at the top of sloping pastures. On clear days the extensive view west stretches across the plain of the River Trent to Sherwood Forest and the smudge of the distant Peak District. The walk now follows this path just below the lip of the edge through a series of hedge-gaps or kissing-gates to reach the edge of a copse. Use the kissing-gate on the left here and walk across the paddock to a cottage, where a gate leads into a tarred lane here in Boothby Graffoe.

At the junction, go ahead along Main Street, walking through the pretty village to a sharp left bend just before reaching the largely Victorian church. **H** Fork right down the rough lane; use a gap-stile beside a gate to join a wide track past a pond and simply remain on this elevated path beside woodland. It eventually becomes enclosed, bending left and right to emerge, via a kissing-

A distant view of Coleby church on Lincoln Edge

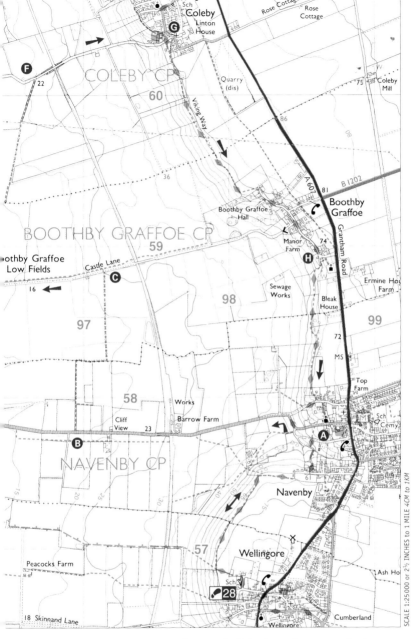

gate and steps, onto a lane in Navenby. Turn left, turn right along an enclosed tarmac path (Cat Walk) towards the church, and the path bends first left and then right to emerge onto a lane by the church. This impressive building dates mainly from the 14th and 15th centuries but was heavily restored in the Victorian era. The west tower was rebuilt in the 18th century after its predecessor collapsed.

Turn left to the start if you began the walk at Navenby. To return to the start of the full walk, turn right past the church and, at a public footpath sign, turn left over a stile **A**. Here you rejoin the outward route and retrace your steps to Wellingore.

Further Information

The National Trust

Anyone who likes visiting places of natural beauty and/or historic interest has cause to be grateful to the National Trust. Without it, many such places would probably have vanished by now.

It was in response to the pressures on the countryside posed by the relentless march of Victorian industrialisation that the trust was set up in 1895. Its founders, inspired by the common goals of protecting and conserving Britain's national heritage and widening public access to it, were Sir Robert Hunter, Octavia Hill and Canon Rawnsley: respectively a solicitor, a social reformer and a clergyman. The latter was particularly influential. As a canon of Carlisle Cathedral and vicar of Crosthwaite (near Keswick), he was concerned about threats to the Lake District and had already been active in protecting footpaths and promoting public access to open countryside. After the flooding of Thirlmere in 1879 to create a large reservoir, he became increasingly convinced that the only effective way to guarantee protection was outright ownership of land.

The purpose of the National Trust is to preserve areas of natural beauty and sites of historic interest by acquisition, holding them in trust for the nation and making them available for public access and enjoyment. Some of its properties have been acquired through purchase, but many have been donated. Nowadays it is not only one of the biggest landowners in the country, but also one of the most active conservation charities, protecting 581,113 acres (253,176 ha) of land, including 555 miles (892km) of coastline, and more than 300 historic properties in England, Wales and Northern Ireland. (There is a separate National Trust for Scotland, which was set up in 1931.)

Furthermore, once a piece of land has come under National Trust ownership, it is difficult for its status to be altered. As a result of parliamentary legislation in 1907, the Trust was given the right to declare its property inalienable, so ensuring that in any subsequent dispute it can appeal directly to parliament.

As it works towards its dual aims of conserving areas of attractive countryside and encouraging greater public access (not easy to reconcile in this age of mass tourism), the Trust provides an excellent service for walkers by creating new concessionary paths and waymarked trails, maintaining stiles and footbridges and combating the ever-increasing problem of footpath erosion.

For details of membership, contact the National Trust at the address on page 94.

The Ramblers' Association

No organisation works more actively to protect and extend the rights and interests of walkers in the countryside than the Ramblers' Association. Its aims are clear: to foster a greater knowledge, love and care of the countryside; to assist in the protection and enhancement of public rights of way and areas of natural beauty; to work for greater public access to the countryside; and to encourage more people to take up rambling as a healthy, recreational leisure activity.

It was founded in 1935 when, following the setting up of a National Council of Ramblers' Federation in 1931, a number of federations in London, Manchester, the Midlands and elsewhere came together to create a more effective pressure group, to deal with such problems as the disappearance or obstruction of footpaths, the prevention of access to open mountain and moorland, and increasing hostility from landowners. This was the era of the mass trespasses, when there were sometimes violent confrontations between ramblers and gamekeepers, especially on the moorlands of the Peak District.

Since then the Ramblers' Association

has played a key role in preserving and developing the national footpath network, supporting the creation of national parks and encouraging the designation and waymarking of long-distance routes.

Our freedom of access to the countryside, now enshrined in legislation, is still in its early years and requires constant vigilance. But over and above this there will always be the problem of footpaths being illegally obstructed, disappearing through lack of use, or being extinguished by housing or road construction.

It is to meet such problems and dangers that the Ramblers' Association exists and represents the interests of all walkers. The address to write to for information on the Ramblers' Association and how to become a member is given on page 95.

Walkers and the Law

The *Countryside and Rights of Way Act 2000 (CRoW)* extends the rights of access previously enjoyed by walkers in England and Wales. Implementation of these rights began on 19 September 2004. The Act amends existing legislation and for the first time provides access on foot to certain types of land – defined as mountain, moor, heath, down and registered common land.

Where You Can Go
Rights of Way
Prior to the introduction of *CRoW* walkers could only legally access the countryside along public rights of way. These are either 'footpaths' (for walkers only) or 'bridleways' (for walkers, riders on horseback and pedal cyclists). A third category called 'Byways open to all traffic' (BOATs), is used by motorised vehicles as well as those using non-mechanised transport. Mainly they are green lanes, farm and estate roads, although occasionally they will be found crossing mountainous area.

Rights of way are marked on Ordnance Survey maps. Look for the green broken lines on the Explorer maps, or the red dashed lines on Landranger maps.

The term 'right of way' means exactly what it says. It gives a right of passage over what, for the most part, is private land. Under pre-CRoW legislation walkers were required to keep to the line of the right of way and not stray onto land on either side. If you did inadvertently wander off the right of way, either because of faulty map reading or because the route was not clearly indicated on the ground, you were technically trespassing.

Local authorities have a legal obligation to ensure that rights of way are kept clear and free of obstruction, and are signposted where they leave metalled roads. The duty of local authorities to install signposts extends to the placing of signs along a path or way, but only where the authority considers it necessary to have a signpost or waymark to assist persons unfamiliar with the locality.

The New Access Rights
Access Land
As well as being able to walk on existing rights of way, under the new legislation you now have access to large areas of open land. You can of course continue to use rights of way footpaths to cross this land, but the main difference is that you can now lawfully leave the path and wander at will, but only in areas designated as access land.

Where to Walk
Areas now covered by the new access rights – Access Land – are shown on Ordnance Survey Explorer maps bearing the access land symbol on the front cover.

'Access Land' is shown on Ordnance Survey maps by a light yellow tint surrounded by a pale orange border. New orange coloured 'i' symbols on the maps will show the location of permanent access information boards installed by the access authorities.

Restrictions
The right to walk on access land may lawfully be restricted by landowners. Landowners can, for any reason, restrict

Countryside Access Charter

Your rights of way are:

- public footpaths – on foot only. Sometimes waymarked in yellow
- bridleways – on foot, horseback and pedal cycle. Sometimes waymarked in blue
- byways (usually old roads), most 'roads used as public paths' and, of course, public roads – all traffic has the right of way

Use maps, signs and waymarks to check rights of way. Ordnance Survey Explorer and Landranger maps show most public rights of way

On rights of way you can:

- take a pram, pushchair or wheelchair if practicable
- take a dog (on a lead or under close control)
- take a short route round an illegal obstruction or remove it sufficiently to get past

You have a right to go for recreation to:

- public parks and open spaces – on foot
- most commons near older towns and cities – on foot and sometimes on horseback
- private land where the owner has a formal agreement with the local authority

In addition you can use the following by local or established custom or consent, but ask for advice if you are unsure:

- many areas of open country, such as moorland, fell and coastal areas, especially those in the care of the National Trust, and some commons
- some woods and forests, especially those owned by the Forestry Commission
- country parks and picnic sites
- most beaches
- canal towpaths
- some private paths and tracks Consent sometimes extends to horse-riding and cycling

For your information:

- county councils and London boroughs maintain and record rights of way, and register commons
- obstructions, dangerous animals, harassment and misleading signs on rights of way are illegal and you should report them to the county council
- paths across fields can be ploughed, but must normally be reinstated within two weeks
- landowners can require you to leave land to which you have no right of access
- motor vehicles are normally permitted only on roads, byways and some 'roads used as public paths'

---

access for up to 28 days in any year. They cannot however close the land:

- on bank holidays;
- for more than four Saturdays and Sundays in a year;
- on any Saturday from 1 June to 11 August; or
- on any Sunday from 1 June to the end of September.

They have to provide local authorities with five working days' notice before the date of closure unless the land involved is an area of less than five hectares or the closure is for less than four hours. In these cases landowners only need to provide two hours' notice.

Whatever restrictions are put into place on access land they have no effect on

existing rights of way, and you can continue to walk on them.

Dogs

Dogs can be taken on access land, but must be kept on leads of two metres or less between 1 March and 31 July, and at all times where they are near livestock. In addition landowners may impose a ban on all dogs from fields where lambing takes place for up to six weeks in any year. Dogs may be banned from moorland used for grouse shooting and breeding for up to five years.

In the main, walkers following the routes in this book will continue to follow existing rights of way, but a knowledge and understanding of the law as it affects walkers, plus the ability to distinguish access land marked on the maps, will enable anyone who wishes to depart from paths that cross access land either to take a shortcut, to enjoy a view or to explore.

General Obstructions

Obstructions can sometimes cause a problem on a walk and the most common of these is where the path across a field has been ploughed over. It is legal for a farmer to plough up a path provided that it is restored within two weeks. This does not always happen and you are faced with the dilemma of following the line of the path, even if this means treading on crops, or walking round the edge of the field. Although the later course of action seems the most sensible, it does mean that you would be trespassing.

Other obstructions can vary from overhanging vegetation to wire fences across the path, locked gates or even a cattle feeder on the path.

Use common sense. If you can get round the obstruction without causing damage, do so. Otherwise only remove as much of the obstruction as is necessary to secure passage.

If the right of way is blocked and cannot be followed, there is a long-standing view that in such circumstances there is a right to deviate, but this cannot wholly be relied on. Although it is accepted in law that highways (and that includes rights of way) are for the public service, and if the usual track is impassable, it is for the general good that people should be entitled to pass into another line. However, this should not be taken as indicating a right to deviate whenever a way becomes impassable. If in doubt, retreat.

Report obstructions to the local authority and/or the Ramblers' Association.

 Global Positioning System (GPS)

What is GPS?

GPS is a worldwide radio navigation system that uses a network of 24 satellites and receivers, usually hand-held, to calculate positions. By measuring the time it takes a signal to reach the receiver, the distance from the satellite can be estimated. Repeat this with several satellites and the receiver can then use triangulation to establish the position of the receiver.

How to use GPS with Ordnance Survey mapping

Each of the walks in this book includes GPS co-ordinate data that reflects the walk position points on Ordnance Survey maps.

GPS and OS maps use different models for the earth and co-ordinate systems, so when you are trying to relate your GPS position to features on the map the two will differ slightly. This is especially the case with height, as the model that relates the GPS global co-ordinate system to height above sea level is very poor.

When using GPS with OS mapping, some distortion – up to 16ft (5m) – will always be present. Moreover, individual features on maps may have been surveyed only to an accuracy of 23ft (7m) (for 1:25000 scale maps), while other features, e.g. boulders, are usually only shown schematically.

In practice, this should not cause undue difficulty, as you will be near enough to your objective to be able to spot it.

How to use the GPS data in this book

There are various ways you can use the GPS data in this book.

1. Follow the route description while checking your position on your receiver when you are approaching a position point.

2. You can also use the positioning information on your receiver to verify where you are on the map.

3. Alternatively, you can use some of the proprietary software that is available. At the simple end there is inexpensive software, which lets you input the walk positions (waypoints), download them to the gps unit and then use them to assist your navigation on the walks.

The Humber Bridge

At the upper end of the market Ordnance Survey maps are available in electronic form. Most come with software that enables you to enter your walking route onto the map, download it to your gps unit and use it, alongside the route description, to follow the route.

 ## Walking Safety

Although the reasonably gentle countryside that is the subject of this book offers no real dangers to walkers at any time of the year, it is still advisable to take sensible precautions and follow certain well-tried guidelines.

Always take with you both warm and waterproof clothing and sufficient food and drink. Wear suitable footwear, such as strong walking boots or shoes that give a good grip over stony ground, on slippery slopes and in muddy conditions. Try to obtain a local weather forecast and bear it in mind before you start. Do not be afraid to abandon your proposed route and return to your starting point in the event of a sudden and unexpected deterioration in the weather.

All the walks described in this book will be safe to do, given due care and respect, even during the winter. Indeed, a crisp, fine winter day often provides perfect walking conditions, with firm ground underfoot and a clarity unique to this time of the year. The most difficult hazard likely to be encountered is mud, especially when walking along woodland and field paths, farm tracks and bridleways – the latter in particular can often get churned up by cyclists and horses. In summer, an additional difficulty may be narrow and overgrown paths, particularly along the edges of cultivated fields. Neither should constitute a major problem provided that the appropriate footwear is worn.

 ## Useful Organisations

Campaign to Protect Rural England
128 Southwark Street, London SE1 0SW
Tel. 020 7981 2800
www.cpre.org.uk

Forestry Commission England
Great Eastern House, Tenison Road,
Cambridge CB1 2DU
Tel. 01233 314546
www.forestry.gov.uk

Lincolnshire County Council
County Offices, Newland, Lincoln LN1 1YL
Tel. 01522 552055
www.lincolnshire.gov.uk

Lincolnshire Wolds AONB
Navigation Warehouse
Riverhead Road,
Louth LN11 0DA
Tel. 01507 609740
www.lincswolds.org.uk

Long Distance Walkers' Association
www.ldwa.org.uk

National Trust
Membership and general enquiries:
PO Box 39, Warrington WA5 7WD
Tel. 0870 458 4000
www.nationaltrust.org.uk

East Midlands Regional Office:
Clumber Park Stableyard,
Worksop, Nottinghamshire S80 3BE
Tel. 01909 486411

Natural England
Block 7 Government Buildings,
Chalfont Drive, Nottingham, NG8 3SN
Tel. 0115 929 1191
www.naturalengland.org.uk

Ordnance Survey
Romsey Road, Maybush,
Southampton SO16 4GU
Tel. 08456 05 05 05 (Lo-call)
www.ordnancesurvey.co.uk

Ramblers' Association
2nd Floor, Camelford House,
87–90 Albert Embankment,
London SE1 7TW
Tel. 020 7339 8500

Public Transport in Lincolnshire
Ring Traveline on 0871 200 2233 or visit
www.lincolnshire.gov.uk/busrailtravel

Tourist Information
www.visitlincolnshire.com
*Local tourist information centres (*not
open all year):*
*Alford: 01507 462143
Boston: 01205 356656
Brigg: 01652 657053
Cleethorpes: 01472 323111
Gainsborough: 01427 676666
Grantham: 01476 406166
Grimsby: 01472 342422
*Horncastle: 01507 526636
Lincoln: 01522 873213/873256
Louth: 01507 609289
Mablethorpe: 01507 474939
Scunthorpe: 01724 297354
Skegness: 01754 899887
Sleaford: 01529 414294
Spalding: 01775 725468
Stamford: 01780 755611
*Woodhall Spa: 01526 353775

Youth Hostels Association
Trevelyan House,
Dimple Road,

Matlock, Derbyshire DE4 3YH
Tel. 0870 770 8868
www.yha.org.uk

 ## Ordnance Survey maps of Lincolnshire

The area of Lincolnshire is covered by
Ordnance Survey 1:50 000 (1¼ inches to
1 mile or 2cm to 1km) scale Landranger
map sheets 112, 113, 120, 121, 122, 129,
130, and 131. These all-purpose maps are
packed with information to help you
explore the area and show viewpoints,
picnic sites, places of interest and caravan
and camping sites.

To examine the area in more detail and
especially if you are planning walks,
Ordnance Survey Explorer maps at
1:25 000 (2½ inches to 1 mile or 4cm to
1km) scale are ideal:

234 (Rutland Water)
235 (Wisbech & Peterborough North)
247 (Grantham)
248 (Bourne & Heckington)
249 (Spalding & Holbeach)
261 (Boston)
271 (Newark-on-Trent)
272 (Lincoln)
273 (Lincolnshire Wolds South)
274 (Skegness, Alford & Spilsby)
280 (Isle of Axholme)
281 (Ancholme Valley)
282 (Lincolnshire Wolds North)
283 (Louth & Mablethorpe)
284 (Grimsby, Cleethorpes & Immingham)

To get to the Lincolnshire area use the
Ordnance Survey OS Travel Map-Route
Great Britain at 1:625 000 (1 inch to 10
miles or 4cm to 25km) scale or OS Travel
Map-Road 5 (East Midlands and East
Anglia including London) or Road Map 8
(South East England including London) at
1:250 000 (1 inch to 4 miles or 1cm to
2.5km) scale.

Ordnance Survey maps are available
from most booksellers, stationers and
newsagents.

www.totalwalking.co.uk

www.totalwalking.co.uk
is the official website of the Jarrold
Pathfinder and Short Walks guides. This
interactive website features a wealth of
information for walkers – from the latest
news on route diversions and advice from
professional walkers to product news, free
sample walks and promotional offers.

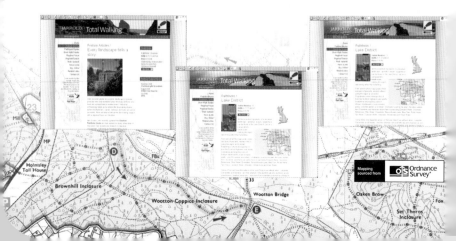